Happy Ever After
Surviving and thriving with a partner

by Hugh Buckingham
Series editor: Joan King

Written by Hugh Buckingham

Series editor: Joan King

Cover design by Phillip Vernon

The editor and publishers gratefully acknowledge permission to reproduce the following material:

The extract from *Letter To Daniel: Despatches From The Heart* by Fergal Keane reprinted on page 56 is reproduced with the permission of BBC Worldwide Limited. Copyright © Fergal Keane 1996.

The extract from *Iris: A Memoir* by John Bayley reprinted on page 72: Duckworth Publishers, London, and St Martins Press, New York. Permission sought.

Published by:
National Christian Education Council
1020 Bristol Road
Selly Oak
Birmingham
B29 6LB

British Cataloguing-in-Publication Data:
A catalogue record for this book is available from the British Library.

ISBN 0-7197-0979-2

First published 1999

©1999 Hugh Buckingham

Typeset by the National Christian Education Council
Printed by Biddles, Guildford, UK

Contents

Preface

*H*appy *Ever After* belongs to a series of books called *Family Change* that is being published by the National Christian Education Council as part of its *Faith in the Future* initiative. Each book in the series focuses on different change-points that many families experience. This one explores ways in which marriages might be nurtured and sustained. The book also considers the relatively new phenomenon of cohabitation and suggests ways in which formal marriages recognized by Church and State and informal marriages or committed cohabitation are both similar and different.

There are more weddings in Britain than in most other European countries, and also, sadly, there are more divorces. Weddings are big business and they are popular. There are wedding exhibitions where we learn that a good wedding costs thousands of pounds and takes up to two years to plan. Fortunately it is possible to marry without such great expense. But after the wedding or the setting up of a home the years stretch ahead; perhaps thirty, forty, fifty and even sixty years is not uncommon. A lot is required of the couple as they grow through the years and face whatever life throws at them.

Most couples marry with high hopes; others enter a committed partnership without the recognition of marriage but they hope to stay together. Staying together is hard work because it is the stuff of human relationships and sometimes expectations exceed what is possible. There is a lot of pressure on the couple relationship in western societies where couplehood is separated from a wider friendship network or community.

This book is for couples who have entered a committed relationship and who want to make it last, indeed not just to sustain a marriage or cohabitation but to thrive in it. And it is important to remember that far more marriages do last than break up, even though the trends are towards shorter-lasting relationships.

The author, Hugh Buckingham, writes with sensitivity and insight. He draws on years of experience as a husband, father and RELATE counsellor and as an Anglican priest with a heavy involvement in social responsibility. His heart for people runs through his writing as he explores the issues and grounds them with stories, case studies and illustrations, sometimes from the Bible. Throughout he gives clues and ideas for nurturing and sustaining the relationship, sometimes with a dash of fun, and he engages the reader in some practical activities that, I am sure, will enrich their own understanding and lives.

Hugh not only uses stories but he challenges readers to recognize their own stories, the ones that they bring to their partnerships and that influence the making of a new story together. The making of this new story is something that the couple set out to do when they commit to one another. It is one that they will continue to develop and, like all good stories, it will have its twists and turns and be unique to the couple. This book is offered as a support to couples who are continuing to create their stories and its message is that, despite everything, life together can be long-lasting and a meaningful route towards greater wholeness and freedom.

Joan King

Series Editor

Introduction

If you are sincerely intent upon sustaining a permanent, lifelong relationship then there are many witnesses from the past and in the present to the joys and deep satisfaction that such a relationship can bring. Yet I must also begin by saying that I think you are undertaking a very brave exercise. There is no relationship that makes so many demands, none that will reveal to us more clearly in all its stark reality the very nature of our being.

So whether you are in a first or a subsequent marriage, whether or not you have children of your own, whether you are struggling with step-children and the confusions that previous marriages can bring, this book is for you. It is a modest attempt to lay bare the nature of such a relationship, to indicate some areas which most of us find difficult and to suggest some strategies that many have found helpful.

As you would expect from this publisher, the book is written from a Christian perspective. I hope that this will not mean that those who are practising Christians will have too high a theological expectation of what I say or that those who rarely set foot in a church will anticipate any hard preaching. The marriage service of the Church of England describes marriage as 'a gift of God in creation', meaning that marriage is a gift to the whole of creation and not just to Christians. The experience of faith in Jesus Christ may well alter our perspective on marriage but the raw material of relationship is the same for everybody. All of us, therefore, whatever our beliefs or lack of them, should be able to find common cause in unravelling the nature of a permanent relationship.

One further thing I should like to add by way of introduction, and that is: if you read the book at all, you should read the whole of it. Any author of course hopes that his book will be read in its entirety but I do not make this suggestion for that self-regarding reason. Rather I believe that there are instincts in all of us that want, even need, to avoid the uncomfortable. If we come to a chapter and decide to skip it, it may be because it is 'old hat' or we just find it uninteresting. That's fine. On the other hand it may also be that we are shying away instinctively from an area of our life which we find most difficult.

For example, suppose you come to the chapter on 'Money and Jobs' and think to yourself, 'I think I'll give that a miss'. The reason could be that you and your partner have been brought up in different patterns; he was always taught to be careful, to keep accounts, to save and so on, while in her family money was always treated in a carefree fashion. This issue may not have been resolved between you; you quarrel about it and therefore avoid the minefields. Or perhaps the arguments are about jobs. You have a two-career partnership and child-care is causing hair-raising problems. It would be nice to think that in these cases we would make a particular effort to see what the chapter had to say. But alas! We are not always so rational. So I simply say, be wary.

At some stage in each chapter I make some practical suggestions. These might be activities, like seeing a film, reading a book or simply points for discussion or questions and answers. Here and there I give resources that you might find valuable. Use any or all of these as you choose. They are not a form of examination, rather an aid to clarifying your mind. However, if you do use them, you will probably find them most helpful if you do them with your partner and some of them even with your children. So here's the first of them.

To do
Discuss it together
When you have read the book, invite your partner to read it as well. Then discuss together anything that comes out of it for you both.

Married or Living Together

The Government and the Opposition parties are at the moment actively promoting marriage as the better way for partners to relate to one another. Christians are naturally pleased about this because they have always seen marriage as the God-intended way for a man and a woman to live together. We shall see some of the reasons for this later on.

It may be that this alliance of the political parties will, in due course, have some effect upon the number of those who get married. But the stark fact is that the number of people who live together without any marriage ceremony is rising fast. According to figures for England and Wales from the Government Actuary's Department, quoted in *The Guardian* on 9th January 1999, 66% of men and 61% of women were married in 1981, whereas today the figures stand at 54% of men and 52% of women. If the present trends continue, the figures are destined to slip to 45% and 44% respectively by the year 2021.

Of course this may not happen. Couples may come to value some of that reassuring stability which marriage, at its best, offers adults and their children too. Fears about the security of children in their formative years are widespread, and though many unmarried couples make as good an attempt at rearing children as their married friends, sometimes even their own children wonder what it is that prevents their parents from getting married.

What is Marriage?

So we need to make some attempt now at facing the issues of cohabitation and marriage. And the first question that will arise, as soon as we put our minds to it, is: What exactly is a marriage? From the outward appearance of two families with children, one married and the other permanently cohabiting, there is scarcely any difference to be seen. So is marriage simply acquiring what some people describe as 'a bit of paper' and therefore of no importance at all?

That is certainly not the way the State sees it, even when it has historically sat most lightly to marriage. As far as the State is concerned, even when the Church acts as its agent, marriage is always a civic ceremony that has clear consequences for the couple involved. Certain tax allowances are only given to married couples. The legal rights of an unmarried father over the children his partner bears were in 1998 just about harmonized with those of a married man, but where inheritance is concerned there are still stark differences. Marriage is a civic status and the State, ever since the 1753 Marriage Act, has taken great care to ensure that each marriage is properly documented and accredited. If the couple go abroad to get married, as a fair number do nowadays, the State will still insist that the ceremonies are conducted in accordance with the laws of each foreign country and are duly recorded when they reach home.

Furthermore, if a couple decide that, once married, they wish to get divorced, the State becomes prominent once again. Lawyers are involved since the couple is dissolving a legal status. These days, the State might even require the couple to seek the services of a conciliator, not so much to try to repair the marriage as to ensure that the divorce goes through with least damage to everybody, especially the children. The financial security for all those involved is safeguarded as far as possible.

But leaving the State out of it—which is easy enough to do during the bulk of our marriages—we need to look at what exactly it is that constitutes a marriage. And in the Western world that which brings about a marriage has always been, whether inside or outside the Church, the uninhibited consent of an adult couple to live together for the rest of their lives. The parish priest or the civil registrar is present, not to bring about the marriage, but to preside over the ceremony of consent and to act as a witness to it. Thus it used to happen in the Middle Ages, and later in the eighteenth century before the Church and State really got tough about it, that couples would engage in an informal ceremony. They would make their vows before informal witnesses in an informal setting (sometimes the local inn) and would thereafter firmly assent, 'We are married before God'. And though more formal arrangements were strongly urged by Church and State, and doubtless by parents too, there was at the time little in the end that any of them could do, since consent was at the basis of the contract.

So we come back to the personal relationship and ask again what it is that makes a marriage on a personal level, and how it differs from cohabitation.

A Public Celebration

Preparations for a wedding are nearly always complex and, more often than not, expensive. It is a day of celebration when a couple strive to look their best. Hospitality to a wide range of friends and the families on both sides is expected and gladly given. People want to have a party because it is a joyous day and everybody should share it. True, the celebrations these days can be somewhat extravagant and few people realize that it is possible to become validly married in quite a simple ceremony. But that is hardly the point. People have an extravagant occasion because they feel extravagantly about it. It is a public statement about their new status. We easily underestimate how important it is for couples to celebrate publicly. It is important not only because it enables them to take their proper place in a society where marriage is still the more usual way of conducting relationships. The other side of it is that the families too can, so to speak, rearrange themselves around the new family. It is definitely a new family, accepted as such now by everybody involved in it. This reduces anxieties about how to relate to them, or indeed about their relatedness.

It is part of the curiosity of cohabitees that their families can be not too sure how to relate to them, especially if they have children. The couple's parents are clearly grandparents when children arrive but it is not too obvious whether they are in-laws or not. In fact, strictly they are not in-laws at all. Presumably the children have uncles, aunts and cousins, but they are not certainly so. In due course everybody shakes down into some kind of working relationship but it makes for an awkward period. And the fact is that the 'private' marriage of cohabitation, if it can be called so, is a very recent arrival upon the scene in this country, and in most other countries of the world, and nobody can quite foresee yet what effect it might have upon wider society.

An Emphatic Endorsement of Marriage

A second issue in the marriage/cohabitation debate in a Christian setting is that Jesus was, according to the Gospels, extremely emphatic about the status of a permanent relationship. When he was asked about the position of married couples in a society which permitted a man to divorce his wife he said, 'In the beginning, at the time of creation, "God made them male and female", as the scripture says. "And for this reason a man will leave his father and mother and unite with his wife, and the two will become one." So they are no longer two, but one. Man must not separate, then, what God has joined together' (*Mark 10.6–9*). (The words inside the double inverted commas are from the Old Testament; Jesus is quoting.)

Now we must recognize that Jesus lived in a society whose culture was very different from ours. One of the most conspicuous differences was the position of women. Although there are a number of formidably active women in the Old Testament, the fact is that in relation to men they were seen to be possessions. You remember the tenth commandment, 'You shall not covet your neighbour's house, nor his wife ... nor anything that is his' (*Exodus 20.17*). A wife was one of a man's possessions and he could therefore divorce her, sometimes for quite paltry reasons, simply by giving her 'a note of dismissal'. No such permission was ever given to wives, who were not in the position of being able to initiate divorce.

In spite of this, Jesus did not easily fall in with the customs of the day. His treatment of women was conspicuously even-handed. He had a band of women around him who offered him all the hospitality he needed. He talked with women freely and comfortably, sometimes scandalizing everybody, including his disciples, by conversing with women on his own or by allowing them physical contact with him. He was certainly unconventional in his day.

A further caution when reading texts from the Bible is that we need to recognize that they cannot be read as if they can be applied directly to a modern situation. There has to be an intervening process of thoughtful interpretation, an aspect of which is always the recognition that the world moves on. After all it is hard enough to make any sense of some of the customs of foreign countries in our own day, let alone one that existed two thousand years ago.

Yet all these cautions do not undermine the sense of urgency in Jesus' words. Clearly they were quite startling for his contemporaries who had never before given such prominence to the married state. Jesus was saying with unexpected passion that they had underestimated the importance of the marriage relationship. The Church today, after centuries of experience, still unequivocally endorses that position. Whatever your own view of that, it is not an argument to be lightly dismissed, especially from one so keen to establish the equal status of women against the customs of his own culture.

Moving from Cohabitation to Marriage

There is a third issue about marriage and cohabitation that is really quite hard to put into words. Perhaps the easiest place to start from is our personal experience. You may have known couples, as so many of us have, who have been cohabiting quite cheerfully for some years and then, maybe because they want to have a child or for other more incoherent reasons, decide that they want to get married. And after a few months of marriage the relationship dissolves.

It seems so odd that what they themselves might describe as 'simply a bit of paper' should have such drastic effects. There is no obvious, outward change in their manner of life. They still live in the same house, go to work, make love, enjoy their friends. So what has changed?

There are elements, I suppose, of the sense of now being trapped for life. 'Till death us do part' is a very long time for most people these days and the prospect of being tied to one person without any let-out, save divorce, can be unexpectedly daunting. Maybe it is a step into respectability, into an ordered world where personal relationships can often take second place to demands from the wider society. It can be irritating to mix with people who, now that the couple are married, do not take the love between them with the seriousness they once did.

But the kernel of it, I believe, lies elsewhere. The act of marriage signals an internal shift. I will be saying more about this in the next chapter. Here it is enough to say that, when people make a decision to cohabit, it is a deliberate move away from their families. They are saying that they are adults now, able and willing to make their own decisions, prepared to live with somebody from another family in order to make a new life together. It is always in some measure an escape into freedom, a decision to be no longer bound by old ties. In a way it is a move into adulthood.

So long as the cohabitation continues, this sense of freedom remains. It is not only the freedom to leave the relationship if it does not work out, though that is there as well. It is more, I believe, the freedom from what lies in the past.

As soon as the cohabitation turns into marriage, however, each partner, maybe without much conscious recognition of the fact, makes a small internal shift back into the family from which he or she comes. They are now properly family, properly married, properly potential or actual parents. And that is where they came from, with all the joys and the stresses that are the largest part of their personal history. And of course, they are different joys and stresses for each partner, because what is always taken for granted in one of their families of origin is seen as somewhat bizarre in the other. So a pair of lovers suddenly shifts into being a married couple and each begins to repeat old patterns. It may be an instinctive fear of this happening and a strong desire not to repeat the pattern of a dysfunctional family of origin that compels some couples never to get married at all.

A simplistic example of the shift I am talking about might be the young couple who set up house together with a shared mortgage. Each has a satisfying full-time job and they have no children. They share the housework and most of the cooking when they get home in the evening. Then they decide to be married. All goes well for a few weeks until the husband comes home one day, tired, and says, 'Where's my tea?' 'What do you mean, where's my tea?' she says indignantly, but he ignores the implications of the remark because this is what happened where he came from—his mother prepared the meals. Now he is in a 'proper family', so the woman makes the tea.

Usually the shifts in behaviour are subtler than that which means that each partner finds it that much harder to get a handle on what is happening between them. But it can make a powerful distinction between cohabiting and being married.

New Pressures on Marriage

There is then, so I believe, a good case to be made for distinguishing cohabitation from marriage, nor is the Christian commitment to marriage untenable in a modern society. But it is unquestionable that there are very much greater pressures upon the married relationship in our own generation and I would like to end this chapter by mentioning a few of them.

The obvious one is that we all live much longer than we used to. Golden weddings these days are two a penny. A hundred years ago they were cause for great wonder. In fact, curiously, the average length of a marriage today is exactly the same as it was at the end of the last century, about twenty years. But marriages then were ended by death while marriages today are ended mainly by divorce. When we contemplate twenty years together it seems a reasonable time, but forty, fifty or sixty years leaves so much more time for relationships to sour or for boredom to set in. This can be hard to bear, particularly in the contemplation of it.

Another pressure upon marriage comes from the advent of reliable artificial contraception. Naturally there were contraceptive devices widely available in earlier times, such as the Victorian era. But the contraceptive pill is barely fifty years old and its high reliability in preventing conception is causing a massive change—of which we have only just begun to see the consequences, not only in sexual relationships but also in the position of women in our society.

It may sound odd to say that artificial contraception is a pressure upon marriage when it is so obviously a wonderful blessing as well. It frees couples to explore their personal, physical, loving union while setting on one side for the time being their desire for children. I have only to mention the fact, for example, that my own great-great-grandmother had twenty-four children, of whom seventeen survived, to show what a marvellous release reliable contraception has been for married couples.

But reliable contraception also makes it a great deal easier to have sexual intercourse outside marriage without much fear of bringing an unwanted child into the world. Undoubtedly this fear was in part a major inhibition to married people seeking out other sexual partners while still remaining married. The temptations have always been there, but now they are, at least with respect to unwanted children, trouble-free.

The last factor I want to mention that makes marriage so much more hazardous these days is that most couples now expect to find personal fulfilment within their relationship. I am far from saying that all couples in the past failed to find a rewarding friendship with their spouse or that love and sexual ecstasy are modern inventions. A long history in East and West of love poetry, of erotic art and of wonderful tales of devoted couples, going back well over a couple of thousand years, gives the lie to that. No, my point is rather that the institution of marriage, and the prior state of cohabitation, bear the weight today of very high expectations. Each partner anticipates that together they will provide nearly everything that will satisfy each other's deepest needs. Expectations of love are not shared out among the wider family as they once were. But it is rarely possible for one person to fulfil the hopes and aspirations of another, so disappointment creeps in. And that is all very sad, because a close partnership is one of the most delightful experiences we are ever offered on this earth, provided we understand that none of us can bear that weight all on our own.

Having made some attempt to face the issues of marriage and cohabitation, and thus to have shown that what I have to say is applicable to any kind of couple, I would like to take you back to the time when you were at home with your family of origin.

To do

Married or Cohabiting: a List

Make a list of all your friends and relations on each side of your family. Put a note alongside their names saying whether they are married or cohabiting. If they are divorced, then note whether they are re-married or re-cohabiting. Do you detect any differences in the groups? Are there any lessons to be learned?

Talk to Your Opposite

If you are married, talk to a cohabiting couple about issues raised in this chapter. If you are cohabiting, talk to a married couple.

Where We Come From

Now I fear you might think this is a curious place to begin. 'Don't we want to be looking forward rather than looking back? After all,' some of you might say, 'I got married to get away from all that and the last thing I want to do is to go back there again!'

I have some sympathies with that view. We all meet people who spend their time living in the past, and the older we become the more likely we are to revel in 'the good old days'. Since I believe strongly that the richness of living is nearly always to be found in what is happening at the moment, I do not advocate dwelling back there. But I do believe that our past is an exceptionally valuable place to discover all kinds of useful information about our present, as many people have discovered already. An illustration from nature might make clear what I mean.

A New Garden Shrub

You decide to plant a new shrub in your garden. You plan where it will go, buy it from the garden centre and put it in. You then watch it grow. How it grows, and what sort of specimen it becomes will depend upon factors like these:

- The degree of healthiness of the shrub itself when you buy it.
- Whether you have chosen a shrub that is right for the climate in your garden.
- How well you prepare the ground, adding the compost and fertilizer.
- Whether it grows up shaded by trees, other shrubs or buildings.
- Whether it gets enough water and proper feeding, particularly in the early years.
- How far you watch it carefully to nip pests and diseases in the bud.

After five or six years a garden expert will be able to come along and make a good guess as to what has happened to the shrub since you planted it. The expert might say, 'That's been planted too close to the wall. You can see how it's leaning away from it. You may need to prop it up', or 'You'll need to feed it some more. You've obviously neglected that a bit'.

That is all recognizable, particularly if you are a gardener. Plants grow according to their prevailing conditions. It is not quite so easy to see that the same sort of principles apply for human beings, that it works the same sort of way. However, it might look like this.

The genetic inheritance from your parents has a powerful, but not completely decisive, effect on the sort of person you become. If your parents could not cope for any reason and you were brought up largely by your grandmother, the climate of that upbringing will have affected you. It will make a difference what sort of stimulation you received when you were young, whether you had a good diet, had satisfactory feeding for your mental and spiritual development. If you grew up overshadowed by a brother or sister, or if one or the other parent favoured them rather than you, it will show today. If, and here the analogy breaks down, you lost one or both of your parents by death or divorce, or a loved sister or brother or grandparent in some way, the heartache will remain and will have its effect upon many of your other close relationships.

Debbie's Story

I think we do understand this instinctively rather better than we think we do. Let me give you a story (which I have invented) and then ask you to ponder the questions at the end of it.

Debbie is twenty-seven years old and has been married for three years. She is the eldest of three children, her brother now being twenty-five and her sister twenty-two. Their mother died when Debbie was thirteen years old. Their father, a somewhat quiet, distant man, was distraught over his wife's death and scarcely talked about it. When Debbie was sixteen, he married a bossy woman whom Debbie did not much care for. She left home as soon as she was eighteen.

- What sort of person do you think Debbie might have married? What clues are there about this in her story?
- What do you think her husband might particularly value in Debbie and therefore what sort of man might he be?
- Who might Debbie be close to in her family?
- What sort of things will Debbie probably always find difficult? ...

The dots are there partly because you might have other questions you want to ask about Debbie but mostly because I would like you to pause before you read on and to see if you can work out what some of the answers might be...

The first thing to say about a story like that, or any other story of a person's upbringing, including your own, is that it is quite impossible to read off answers from any given scenario. Human beings are not machines. They never respond in just the same way to any particular set of events. We are awkward, provoking, strangely unique, unexpected, contrary, changeable, humorous.

There are all kinds of things about Debbie that I have not told you. And if I did tell you a good deal more, e.g. what she looks like and who her friends are, you might still tell me that it is not those things you want to know. Rather you may prefer to know about how she gets on with her brother and sister, and whether she goes out to work. An interpretation of any set of information about anybody is simply that—an interpretation. And some new information and a different interpreter might reach an alternative conclusion. All our conclusions must be contingent, and we must recognize that of all interpreters, in the end, once she has arrived there, the best interpreter of all will be Debbie herself.

A third most important factor to take into consideration whenever we hear anybody's story is this. Our own emotional life has been deeply affected by what in particular has happened to us. All the events of our lives are etched deep in our souls and half the time we really have not a clue what is going on inside there. Everything arrives muddled up. Emotions stack up like planes waiting to land at the airport and one of them suddenly arrives out of the blue, usually when our flight control tower is least prepared for it. So what comes about is that one small item in a story, or the story as a whole, suddenly resonates with something that has happened to us, often without our recognizing the tie-up.

So when you read Debbie's story, the bit that resonates with you perhaps is that you also have a simply ghastly stepmother. Instantly this bit of the story becomes the dominating issue, because it is your issue. That is absolutely fine for as long as you are using Debbie's story for your own purpose. But if there is a real Debbie in front of you, she wants all of her story to be heard and acted upon, not just the bit that makes sense to you. We must always beware of our own experience usurping that of other people.

Nevertheless, with those cautions, there are a fair number of clues in Debbie's story about the sort of relationships she might be having. What sort of man might she have married? Well, we note that between the ages of thirteen and sixteen Debbie was the oldest woman in the family. With her father a distant man, she might well have taken her mother's place for a while, looking after her younger brother and sister, perhaps even running the house for them all. So with such a background she might now be married to rather a quiet man where she takes full control of the household. On the other hand, if she is a different character, she might, with the advent of her stepmother, have rebelled against the whole 'family' bit and taken to herself a wilder character to suit her new mood. But note that she would still be reacting to what happened in her past.

Her husband, contrariwise, might have been seeking the maternal figure that Debbie has it in her to be. On the other hand he might have recognized and enjoyed and ultimately wanted to share her rebellion if she has moved that way. Yet he also has his own family story in the past, and the real complication of a marriage comes when you have to try to unravel two stories which are now intertwined so closely.

Who might Debbie be close to? She's likely to relate well to her brother and sister since she looked after them for three years. We cannot be too sure about her father. She may never have become close to him at all because of his unapproachability and she may have continued to accept that with a shrug of the shoulders. On the other hand, she may have an element of grief in her that she has never had the father she felt she needed, and she could be looking around for somebody to take his place. We do not know how close to her mother she might have been but we do know that her mother died when she was thirteen and that the next woman in her life, her stepmother, supplanted both her mother and her father. So it is possible that she will find it hard to share her confidences with an older woman.

We have already recognized what Debbie might find difficult, i.e. relating to older men and women, avoiding an exclusively maternal role, wondering what has happened to those lost teenage years between thirteen and sixteen when most of us are testing out the world of our parents rather than supporting it, and, if she has not done so already, finding and acknowledging her anger.

Debbie's story will, I hope, have given you some idea of the stark influences from the past that we bring with us to every subsequent relationship. Even when we pick up the general idea and run with it a while, it can still be fiendishly difficult to understand and to interpret our own pasts. We stand too close to ourselves. We cannot gain that necessary distance which enables us to look at facts with some dispassion. If you are in a muddle it is often a good idea to talk through the difficulties with somebody experienced in the field.

Some Common Issues from the Past

What I want to do now at the end of this chapter is to indicate briefly a few of these issues of the past that commonly affect what we become.

Our Position in the Family

Our position in the family always has some influence. If we are the eldest of three, as Debbie is, then we become used to being 'looked up to' by our brother and sister, and sometimes by our parents too. The expectation is that we will be responsible, give an example, do as we are told. Some people who are 'eldests' become docile and co-operative, some quietly seethe and others openly rage against becoming an adult far too early. If we are the youngest then traditionally we are seen as 'spoilt'. Sometimes we are, and our growing-up assumptions therefore are that everybody will love us, and if they do not they must be a fool or a knave. If we are not spoilt at all it might put us in a sulky mood because we feel we ought to be. If we are the middle one of three we are neither one thing nor the other and these children often have strong mood swings or become rather solitary.

A two-child family is nice and neat for the parents and some pairs get along fine. But it only requires a slight preference to be shown by the parents for one or the other for the original jealousies to arise in the form of squabbling carried over into adulthood. Single children, so often absolutely secure in the love of their father and mother, can find it hard to discover a place in the world where their early experiences make sense. And though it sounds from the outside tremendously exciting and rewarding to come from a larger family than three children, many will confess that it is easy to get lost within the family as an individual. It is true that children from big families are often well-placed to relate contentedly to all sorts of people outside the family, though for people who have had this experience, a crowd is often much easier than meeting an individual at a deeper level.

Random Happenings

There is nothing we can do about our place in the family, nor can we do anything but bear a whole lot of other events that just happen to us. A period of severe illness, for example, when we were children, even though we have fully recovered from it, might lead into later habits of dependency. It was good to be looked after and not to have to take any responsibility for ourselves during that time. When we recovered, unconsciously we wanted to retain some of the advantages our illness gave us, in particular the extra special care we received. So a part of us in adulthood easily reverts to being a 'patient' again, and our chosen partner could be somebody whose experience, in their youth, was of having to care for somebody else in the family.

It is not usually comfortable to discover at a fairly young age that we are not as bright as we would like to be. We observe parents and teachers becoming exasperated with us and we quickly retaliate by becoming unco-operative and indifferent. 'To hell with them,' we think. 'If they think we're stupid, then we'll act stupid.' A society which allows league tables to govern the whole of education will breed a proportion of adults whose uniqueness and skills have not been encouraged or even discovered and who will therefore never have felt valued. If we are such a person, or marry such a person, it will be easy to miss the wretched vulnerability that lies not far beneath the bluster and defiance.

Early Losses

Another early trauma, particularly common these days, is the loss of a parent through death or, more usually, divorce. There is a respectable body of opinion that believes that it is less hurtful for a child's parents to divorce than it is for it to suffer their endless bickering and fights. I am inclined not to agree with that opinion, believing that it may have something to do with parents salving their consciences for the hurt their divorce causes the child. It is rare to find a child who encourages their parents to divorce.

The loss of a parent, particularly but not exclusively, in my experience, between the ages of twelve and sixteen when the move from childhood to adulthood is taking place, can have the most powerful effects years and years later. We can carry inside us anger, grief, a keen sense of injustice, a sense of failure, all kinds of emotions that have not been worked through. If we have not ourselves suffered any such misery it is perhaps easier to see how damaging such experiences might be. But it is no less difficult to handle, wherever we come from.

Above is just a sample of the sort of early experiences that couples can encounter within a long-term relationship like marriage. We must not expect at an early stage in our relationship to be able to handle, or even to recognize, those mutual experiences of our youth which are part of that which draws us together in the first place. It is, as I have just said, especially complex because each of us brings to the relationship a life story which is in the process of being worked out, and it is the marriage that bears the brunt of the exposure.

Some of the suggestions below might give you a chance to ponder further upon the question of our pasts and how they influence our presents. Meanwhile, before I come to discussing the issue of intimacy and of all that flows from that, I want to spend one further chapter looking at another outside influence upon our marriages, and that is the families and friends who provide the context for our relationship.

To do

Talk with your Family

When you can get them on their own, talk to one of your brothers or sisters. Ask them what it was like for them in their childhood and as they were growing up. Then ask them how they perceived you. Also try talking to one or both of your parents in the same way. How was it for them bringing you up? Remember that each person you talk to will have rather different memories of you.

Some Professional Help

If you are in a muddle about your past, go and talk it over with a professional counsellor. RELATE will help, or look up 'counsellors' in the Yellow Pages. You do not have to be in a crisis just to go and talk to someone.

A Fascinating Book

Read John Cleese (yes that one!) and Robin Skynner's book *Families and How to Survive Them* (Methuen paperback). It is very easy to read and full of exceptionally funny cartoons.

In-laws and Out-laws

I fear this may be one of the chapters you want to skip. In-laws, particularly mothers-in-law, have a melancholy reputation, encouraged by every stand-up comedian in the country. They are often seen as interfering old tyrants, hell-bent on spoiling the relationship between the partners, determined to poke their nose into every corner of the couple's lives.

In truth many in-laws are not in the least like this and there are countless stories of the selfless devotion that in-laws give partners. But there are very good reasons why the jokes are so widespread. I hope we shall end this chapter having had a more objective look at all the people who surround any relationship, discerning some of the reasons why the reputation of mothers-in-law is so bad and thus putting couples into a comprehensible family context.

Separating from our Family of Origin

But I begin with the sort of statement that is often made by couples, particularly at the outset of their relationship. You might feel you want to say, 'Look, I'm now living with/married to Sue/Tom, and our relationship is absolutely nothing to do with anybody else. We'll live our lives and you can live yours, and we don't want any interference, thank you very much.'

Now I believe that there are senses in which it is right for couples to make that sort of stand, and it may be more important for some couples than for others. I have two reasons for believing this.

In the first place we need to understand that to join permanently with a partner is a very decisive step. It is a deliberate move into what might almost be called foreign territory. Probably each partner has already left home, maybe living in a hostel or sharing a flat, and this can be the decisive, and sometimes painful, break for the parents. But for the young adults the larger step can be when the couple get married or set up house together. The focus of their lives shifts. Maybe they no longer have 'their' bedroom back in the family house. They are at last separate.

It might be particularly necessary to claim this freedom if you come from a family which is very close, either close in a family-friendly sort of way or closed in by strange forces you cannot really get the hang of. The stronger the ties that either sort of family use to bind you to them (not normally by deliberate intent, of course) the more necessary it is that you should make some attempt to unshackle those ties and to begin to become independent. They will fight to keep you 'one of us' and you, while acknowledging with gratitude all you have received from your family, will have to reply, 'Yes, all right, thank you for all of that, but now I'm "one of them" '. But, one of whom? This is my second point. It is not a matter simply of moving over from one family, our own, into another, our partner's. There are always likely to be tensions between those two families of origin and we can only do the best we can in distributing our favours. No, the critical issue is not either of the families we have come from but the entirely new family we are creating by our commitment to each other, a commitment sealed usually by a decision to share a common surname. Here lies the crucial adjustment, an adjustment in our primary loyalties. Our first commitment now is to our partner. It is they in future who will receive our most intimate thoughts and fancies. Our secrets will be their secrets, our hopes and fears theirs. Parents—and this most often happens between mothers and their daughters —will have to become accustomed to no longer being the primary confidante.

It is this adjustment in loyalties which lies behind all the mother-in-law jokes. It is desperately hard for parents to find themselves supplanted in this way. All sensible parents know that they have, as they will say, 'to let their children go', but many are not prepared for this displacement of allegiance, this severance from their child. It can feel like an expulsion, and it cannot be surprising that, particularly at the beginning of a relationship, tensions between partners and parents abound.

There are other family loyalties which new partners will turn their back on. I have called this chapter 'In-laws and Out-laws' because, once we have separated, we will also, probably quite slowly, become out-laws to much of what our family took for granted. We become out-laws not to laws in general but to those particular laws which our parents, either openly or by silent implication, insisted in the past that we live by. It is not that we will necessarily rebel against all that our parents have taught us. Many of us have already done that in our teenage years. Rather we now have the opportunity to set out on new paths that we shall work out over the years with our partner. It will only be over time that we come to recognize that some of those new paths are not in essence all that different from those which our parents taught us all those years ago to love and live by.

Issues of Faith

One of the transitions that we may make concerns our attitude to issues of faith. Our family may have had some greater or lesser attachment to the Church, and, during our junior years at least, we probably went along with that. It may be that as teenagers we discovered a fresh faith for ourselves which our family may not have understood, or we may have drifted away from the practice of any faith as matters of greater urgency lay in wait for us.

It is an issue that we can expect to have to address in our first few years of marriage. Our partner will have brought different experiences into the marriage from his or her family and we need to decide at least what sort of practices we are going to encourage in our children. Sometimes, particularly before the children come along or where there is a little more leisure as the last child goes to school all day, there is an opportunity for experimenting outside the traditional ways. New paths of faith present themselves. I think we need to feel relaxed about this. Jesus was not conspicuous for telling people what to do. He told many stories, and asked lots of questions, many of them open-ended so that people had to make up their own minds. He wanted people to think. He was not interested in disciples who came along for the ride. In the end though he always threw down the challenge of the best way, which he said was to 'Follow me'.

Up till now in this chapter I have talked of the break that a new allegiance will inevitably bring about. I believe strongly that to understand and to begin the practice of this change of loyalties is one of the primary roots of a successful relationship. We cannot expect satisfactorily to love our partner if all that is most precious to us remains with one or more members of our family of origin. Having said that, however, I have to go on to say that we cannot expect to sustain a partnership simply out of the resources we have to offer one another.

Other People in our Marriage

In essence what I mean is that we need other people, just as they need us. Let's look at that first from the point of view of the story of our lives.

Our Families

Where I live, at the top of the stairs we have a dozen or more quite large photographs, each separately framed. They show my wife when she was small, either on her own in pigtails, or with her two brothers. There's me, aged about six, hands in pockets, staring belligerently into the camera, and a year or two on with three of my sisters. My grandmother is there, playing patience as always, and another picture shows my mother with her first child and her own father and grandfather (my great-grandfather). My wife's father appears in another photograph as a boy with his brother and sister. We change the photos around from time to time but this 'Rogues' Gallery' has been part of our lives for many years now. What is it all about?

I believe we just thought of it as a nice idea when we first began it, but I have come to see that it is rather more than that. The 'Rogues' Gallery' places my wife and myself into a historical context. We have come from somewhere. These are real people who have shaped what we have become. They may be wearing the oddest clothes or enjoying some bizarre cultural practices quite outside our own experiences. Half of them we have never known or perhaps have only met occasionally or, even if they are still alive, they cross our paths at weddings and funerals and nowhere much else. Yet without them neither of us would be here and neither would our children. They 'place' us in a continuous story.

This need to find our own personal story creeps up on us as we become older. It is quite hard to see why it becomes increasingly important to many people. It may be there is something about the hard knocks of married life which forces us to see that neither of us can satisfy the other simply on our own. Perhaps more, there is a sense of security in knowing where we have come from. If the future is all too uncertain, at least the past has a shape.

Whatever it is, it is as sure as can be that this hankering to know past histories reflects a fundamental impulse in human life, as can clearly be observed in the habits of young children. For, if they are given the slightest encouragement, many children will ask to see old photo albums if there are any around. 'Who's that?' 'Did I ever meet her?' 'Why is he wearing those funny clothes?' 'That's not really Uncle Tom, is it?' 'Is that my brother who died when he was a baby?' The children will find pictures of themselves and of their parents in earlier years particularly entertaining. So this is what happens to people as they grow up, is the unspoken message. And if they can induce them to do so, children may urge their parents to tell their own stories of what it was like when they were young, and especially all the 'bad' things that they did.

My wife and I are fortunate (and it is only good fortune and nothing else) to have come from families where there were stable marriages on both sides. Children who have been adopted or fostered, or whose parents have divorced, are in a more precarious position when it comes to knowing their roots and family history. If we are not adopted or fostered ourselves, we have nevertheless all read the touching stories of young, or even much older, people discovering the need in themselves to unearth their own birth parents and, once they have done so, many of them feel more settled, more anchored in reality.

The children of divorced parents have even more bewildering experiences. Adopted children can choose to find another parent; the children of divorced parents most often have another parent or parents thrust upon them. They are bound to live with one parent or the other and the conflict of loyalties they experience can be much more acute than many adults realize. Yet their need to 'place' themselves in a comprehensible history is evidenced by a conversation I once had with a lady who was closely involved with a national step-parent organization. In all the years she had been working with the children of divorced parents, she told me, she had never known a child who was unable to state what all the relationships around him or her were with complete accuracy. The adults became confused over who was related to whom but not the children.

So what I have been saying so far is that, although there is a sense in which we rightly make a break with the past when we become married, we throw far too much responsibility on to our marital relationship if we do not draw our own family stories into the new story of our marriage. At the same time we do that, we will find ourselves bringing along with us into the marriage all those people who have shaped and keep shaping us—our parents, our uncles, aunts and cousins, our brothers and sisters and their families. And these people are not simply burdens to be borne (though one or two of them might be!) but rather additional resources for our marriage as well as people to be loved in their own right.

Keith and Maureen's Story

An example might help here. Maureen has been married to Keith for several years and they have two children, now both at school. Keith is becoming ever more moody. He snaps at Maureen and the children and is not much interested in making love any more. He works hard and spends most of his spare time down at the allotment. Maureen nags away at him and keeps saying, 'You're getting just like your dad,' which infuriates Keith. Things are not good.

One day, particularly low, Keith finds himself talking to his elder brother, Dave, about it all. He tells Dave that he has always found their dad harsh and uninterested in him. 'Oh no!' says Dave, 'he's always telling me how much he thinks of you. Don't you know about dad?' 'What about dad?' 'I mean his chronic headaches.' And Keith had never known because dad had never allowed it to be mentioned. His harshness becomes a bit more comprehensible. Keith begins to talk to his dad again, differently this time. Relationships ease. Keith relaxes a bit. And in a month or two Maureen says, 'Hey, Keith, you've changed.' And he grins.

A simple tale—too simple, of course. But you see my point. What Keith is in his marriage is affected by what is happening elsewhere in the family. The clues to undertaking adjustments in his marital relationship lie in an engagement with his family.

So it is not only our own stories which are important. Our families' stories too are intimately bound up with the sort of person we are and the sort of relationships we make. There is a pressing need, for our sake and for theirs, that we aim to keep developing our relationships with our families.

You see, there is a culture of separateness in our country at the moment. People's quite understandable ambition is to find a place of their own, some steps away from their families, and to go and live in it. This is my home, my own place, ours. We can be grateful that we live in a country where the vast majority of people can make this dream come true. It fulfils that element of our marriage that needs to be separate. The downside is that it can create difficulties for maintaining links with our families. No one expects us to return in any foreseeable future to a tribal lifestyle where families gather round one another in a small geographical area. But it remains perilous to think that we can go it alone.

Grandparents and great–grandparents are often of unexpected significance. I have lost count of the number of people I have talked with who, especially if they lack a sustaining relationship with their parents, have found a grandparent a wonderful source of refreshment and security. Naturally it is a good deal easier to be a grandparent than a parent. Grandparents are emotionally at several steps removed from the parent/child relationship, nor do they have to put up with the children for more than a few hours or a week at a time at most. But they can often be the conduit through which love, and committed love, is shown to be available elsewhere than with parents and brothers and sisters alone. Also, since great–grandparents and sometimes grandparents tend to die when the children are young, it gives children an opportunity to discover how love can be maintained even through the misery of loss.

Friendships

Finally here we need to look at the place of friendships in marriage. I suspect we have reached a place in the development of our culture where there is a strong, underlying yearning for friendships with all kinds of different people but not yet much sense of security that enables them to become possible. We both want friends, and friends of both sexes, and at the same time are afraid of the complications that friendships can bring. In his book *An Intimate History of Humanity* (Sinclair-Stevenson, 1994), Theodore Zeldin quotes research from France where large samples of people have been asked what they value most. They have been given a list that includes: family and children; freedom and independence; work; success; money; friendship; sex; and a few more. In each of the polls friendship came very high and in one of them it was top, with 96% valuing it more than any of the other factors listed.

Yet so difficult is friendship in practice that very many married couples take the safe route and seek, or are permitted to seek, friendship only with people of the same sex. Thus women make friends, when their children are small, with other mums that they meet at the health clinic or, later, outside the school gate, while men seek companions down at the leisure centre or join Round Table or other all-male groups. Many such friendships can be very satisfying and their value is often tested when a crisis arises in the family and exposes how many of them are, as we say, fair weather friends.

Couples make friends with other couples and sometimes several couples will go out together. There is safety in numbers. And perhaps this is the place to begin exploring the joys of friendship with both sexes. The more often that we meet people of the other sex in cheerful, unthreatening conditions, the less likely are we to indulge in imaginative fantasies. There's nothing like seeing a man excavate his teeth with a toothpick after a heavy meal for destroying some of our daydreams! But in the end the sober fact is that we can scarcely avoid, and honestly do not need to avoid, after we are married, meeting people whom we find attractive. It is scarcely credible that in twenty, forty or fifty years of marriage we shall never meet such a person. How far we can let them enrich our lives through their friendship without jeopardizing our marriage will depend upon the level of trust that we have forged in our own marriage. I will be coming back to this subject in the chapter on 'Money and Jobs'.

And now we have reached the point when we shall look more closely at what goes on personally between a man and a woman who have decided to throw in their lot with one another. We shall look at intimacy.

To do

Make a Family Tree

If you are inclined that way, make a family tree for both you and your spouse. Do not go too far back at first; your grandparents are probably far enough. Write beside each name, if you like, a couple of words about them, e.g. 'second marriage', 'wonderful friend', 'never met' and so on.

Make Contact

Make contact with a friend or relation you have not seen for a year or two.

Intimacy

The Woman
My lover has the scent of myrrh
    as he lies upon my breasts.
My lover is like the wild flowers
    that bloom in the vineyards at Engedi.

The Man
How beautiful you are, my love;
    how your eyes shine with love!

The Woman
How handsome you are, my dearest;
    How you delight me!
The green grass will be our bed;
    the cedars will be the beams of our house,
and the cypress trees the ceiling.
I am only a wild flower in Sharon,
    a lily in a mountain valley.

The Man
Like a lily among thorns
    is my darling among women.

The Woman
Like an apple tree among the trees of the forest,
    so is my dearest compared with other men.
I love to sit in its shadow,
    and its fruit is sweet to my taste.
He brought me to his banqueting hall
    and raised the banner of love over me.
Restore my strength with raisins
    and refresh me with apples!
    I am weak from passion.
Good News Bible Second Edition © 1994

You may recognize this poem. It comes from a series of poems called the *Song of Songs* and was written several hundred years before the time of Christ. It describes with a delicate eroticism the fire of love that has been ignited between a young unmarried couple and the couple's longing for a permanent bond. It promises that 'love is strong as death, passion fierce as the grave' and that 'many waters cannot quench love, neither can floods drown it. If one offered for love all the wealth of one's house, it would be utterly scorned.'

It comes of course from the Old Testament in the Bible, and how wonderful it is that the joy of love should be so frankly celebrated at the heart of the Church's sacred scriptures! It makes one grateful that the Church's faith is securely founded upon the history and convictions of the Jewish people. For the Jews have always been a race who unashamedly glory in the created earth and everything that God gives us here.

Now I am aware that sexual abandon is not—perhaps fortunately—an endless feature of married life, and that the Church has scarcely been, throughout its history, an enthusiastic supporter of adult passion. I shall come back to both those points in a moment. But it would undermine much that God gives us through the love of a man and a woman if we did not begin a chapter on 'Intimacy' by acknowledging with great happiness the marvels of that relationship.

God fully intends that the sexual act shall lead, from time to time, to the conception of a child and we need to take this purpose with the utmost seriousness, as we shall see in a later chapter. But he also intends that this shall be one of the ways in which love is expressed and shared, in which human beings come as close to becoming 'no longer two, but one', as Jesus described it, as it is possible for two separate people to achieve.

You will have discovered by now, I hope, many a device for nurturing your sexual relationship in the midst of busy working and family lives. You will be aware how easily physical and mental exhaustion can wash over you so that sex flies out of the window. So you will have learned that, while a routine of sexual behaviour can be all that a couple can manage for a time and can therefore be a safeguard of love, in the end routine can have a deadening effect. We need to be inventive where we can, to snatch unexpected times together, to take advantage of temporary absence of the children and friends, and not to be over-solemn. If we can scrape a few pounds together and go off on our own for a night or two that can be very invigorating. We need to make the best of every moment and to revel in the unexpected.

This is not the place to go into further detail. There are dozens of books available, some of which you will no doubt have read, and every general interest magazine under the sun has an article about sex somewhere. You need to keep your wits about you because you cannot take for gospel everything that you read. You should trust your own experience. People's beliefs about human relationships differ and the boundaries that they find acceptable may not be the same as yours. It is all too easy to inject an alien belief or practice into a relationship and thereby upset a delicate balance. Keep talking to one another is the clue.

It is a pity that the Church, very early on in its history, largely surrendered to a negative view of the sexual relationship. There was a small cult of virginity within the surrounding Roman secular society, but the Church took to it with a vengeance. There grew up in the first three or four hundred years of the Church's life a sharp differentiation between the married and the celibate life. The celibate were those who were likely to achieve salvation more surely than those who were married. They did not exactly condemn married life but neither did many of the early teachers enthuse over it. St Paul's saying: 'It is better to marry than to burn' (with passion, that is) was about where they stood.

Heaven knows, none of us is unaware of the dangers of the sexual instinct. Uncontrolled sexuality leads to enormous mental and spiritual hurt at the least and to the most vicious brutality when there are no impediments in place. Every newspaper every day shows us that. But the Church, even today, is still more frightened of the hazards than it is supportive of an awesome gift of God. If you find such a negative attitude in the Church in the area where you live and, perhaps, worship, I hope you will recall that Jesus, the Church's Master, though completely clear about the importance of the married relationship, took a markedly relaxed attitude towards sexual misdemeanours. He reserved his severest strictures for those who stood in condemnation of others.

However, none of us can pretend that sexual intercourse is all that there is to intimacy. We spend far more time simply living together than having sex, and what we are in bed is often more closely related to what we are in the rest of our daily life than we recognize. This is why, if things go wrong between you sexually, it may be more profitable to examine what is going wrong in the remainder of the day than to purchase a whole lot more sex manuals. Manuals are fine but are best read from a position of strength rather than of weakness. Sexual intimacy is fed, or it withers, by what happens between us in other departments of our life, and it is to this that I now want to turn.

Creating a Friendship

One way of looking at this is to think in terms of building a friendship. In a healthy married life of course there will always be more than friendship. Married friends will share an intimacy that other friends do not. Yet some of the characteristics of friendship are shared. I am now going to suggest three areas in which friendship can grow, but these by no means exhaust the possibilities.

Before I discuss them you might like to take a moment to consider for yourself what you take friendship to be. What exactly do you look for in a friend? And how much of that sort of friendship is reflected in your marriage and where would you like to strengthen it?

Friendship in my marriage

The bits that work well

....

....

The bits that work not quite so well

....

....

If you have written anything down there, in the end the consideration of those issues will be far more important than what follows. But at least you might pick up some more hints in what I have to say below.

Listening

This is an obvious beginning. We are not likely to make any progress in any relationship whatever unless we are prepared to give each other attention. It is what we always accuse one another of failing to do. 'You simply haven't heard a word I've said, have you?' 'Uhmh, well … you're on about the children, aren't you…?' 'No, as a matter of fact I was talking about your mother' 'Ah…' Your partner at that moment did not want to give attention to the children, and least of all to mother, so it was easier not to listen.

So let me go on to say immediately that it is neither sensible nor possible to listen to our partner with any seriousness all the time. In our ordinary daily conversations we are mostly concerned with exchanging information, being reasonably helpful to one another and getting the work done. It can be very irritating if your partner is always looking for meanings below the surface. If she says, 'Give me a hand with the washing up, will you please?' and he replies, 'Now I wonder what you're really saying by asking me that?' she might be thinking, 'You lazy so-and-so.' However, this is scarcely the moment to go into all that so she might just say brusquely, 'Here's the tea towel, dick-head.'

This illustrates two different kinds of listening. The first is simply attending to the natural courtesies of the daily round, answering when we are spoken to, always trying to notice what is going on around us and responding one way or another to requests for help. This sort of listening will include hearing the accounts of one another's day which, to be honest, can turn out to be a little tedious, especially if our partner has spent the day largely with people at work we scarcely know. Yet we shall see how important this is when we come to consider the rearing of children in a later chapter.

But the most fruitful sort of listening is when we take time out to concentrate on what is happening under the surface. It is sometimes called 'listening to the music of the words'. It means that we listen not simply to the words that our partner is speaking but to the deeper emotions from which the words are spoken. It is a question of putting myself in the other's shoes, and asking, 'What is s/he really feeling about this?' Oddly, if we give people's emotions this attention, we will often be able to pick up the tiniest, most subtle hints they give us about how they are feeling. A shift of the eyes or a twitch of the lips is often quite enough for us to know that something is up even if we are not at all sure what it is all about. We are much more likely to wish not to pay attention to these underlying emotions than we are not to notice them in the first place.

For the fact is that we are getting close here to the heart of a relationship. What one partner does, or feels, or makes happen, affects intimately the course of the couple's life together. To give close consideration to our partner's feelings will lead in the end to a demand for a shift in behaviour. Lying behind such attention is a series of bids for change, in our partner and in ourselves.

So, for example, Peter has come home from work increasingly moody for the past few weeks. Angela is becoming irritated with him but he will not talk. What is happening is that Peter is being bullied and put down by his boss and has just failed to receive the promotion that he felt he was due. He does not want to raise it all with Angela because he knows she feels he does not have enough confidence in himself. He is also not entirely sure how Angela would cope with him if he became more self-confident because he suspects that she rather likes being in charge at home. So Angela storms at him most evenings and he spats back. But he does not reveal, if he can help it, what is happening at work, partly because he is ashamed of being bullied and partly because he is afraid of upsetting the balance of relationships at home to which they have both become accustomed.

It is not surprising that listening is such hard work.

Encouragement

To speak of people encouraging one another can sound both banal and faintly immoral. It is fairly obvious that people enjoy being encouraged but it may be that rather less of it is practised because we feel people should not need it. It is all right for children, but adults should be mature and self-sufficient. The one who seeks encouragement must in some sense be submissive to, be in the power of, the one who encourages. So embarrassment leads to men and women continuing an effective, and maybe at times boring, task for years without a word of cheer. No wonder the opposite misfortune—discouragement—is so widespread.

Yet encouragement is no shame provided that we take care only to encourage that which is, if only mildly, estimable. It is easy to fall into the habit, once we have understood the value of encouragement, of encouraging virtually everything that happens. It is truly embarrassing if one partner comes back from work and makes mention of some small kindness they were able to do and the other partner, with dancing eyes and joyful mien, greets the news like the arrival of summer. The kindness did not deserve that level of response, and next time the partner will keep mum about what happened at work.

For the central task of encouragement is to pay tribute proportionately, to encourage that which is praiseworthy. Its purpose is to distinguish one sort of behaviour from another. We all know that some of what we do deserves praise and some does not. Once we have heard what is commendable about what we have done it is much easier to listen to the negative.

Suppose your partner comes back from a shopping expedition one afternoon and, a mite shame-facedly, pulls a new coat out of a bag and puts it on. 'Hey there! What do you think of it?' It is your partner's money and neither of you ever minded the other spending a bit on him- or herself, but really! This takes the biscuit. In your view the colour is wrong and does not match anything else in your partner's wardrobe. You cannot imagine on what sort of occasion the coat is going to be worn. So what do you say? 'You can pack that away and take it straight back. It's hideous'? You can imagine the reaction, either a furious onslaught or deep resentment. You have made a direct attack not only on your partner's taste but upon his or her own definition of self. This reaction, which has all the appearance of a commendable honesty, in practice will set up further barriers between you.

You need to reflect that neither you nor your partner can ever be certainly sure that either of you is right or wrong. The purchase could be a mistake or could be a confident shift towards a new image. What you need to find is an approach which is encouraging and at the same time faithful to yourself. And the encouragement needs to come first.

So you might begin by saying, 'It's great that you've bought yourself a coat'. This immediately frees your partner from any guilt that might be carried concerning the purchase and acknowledges that each of you has the right to make decisions for yourselves. You then might continue by giving some attention to the coat to determine what, if anything, you like about it. So you might praise the cut of the shoulders or the fit of the collar or the length. All this needs to be said and can be said without sacrificing your integrity, and the chances are that, while you are saying it, your partner will be looking at you shrewdly and will soon say, 'You don't like it, do you?' S/he has twigged it, as most of us do most of the time. And then you can go on to say that you wonder whether the colour is right and so on, so that the way now lies open for an honest exchange of views, which might or might not end in the coat going back to the shop.

If we have not been used to encouraging one another in this way, or by a simple affirming word or look of gratitude for doing that which we expect each other to do, we might be surprised to discover how captivating such behaviour can become. The 'thank you' for a meal, or for a shelf put up, or for a pair of curtains re-hung, can make all the difference. When partners notice the little things that one does for the other and acknowledge the action then they encourage one another and their relationship is nurtured.

The Use of Touch

My last suggestion concerns the use of touch outside the context of sexual intercourse. And here we must begin by acknowledging that there are excellent reasons for approaching this subject with some diffidence. Three occur to me.

In the first place we must make ourselves consciously aware that some countries and cultures will always act in ways that seem to us unconventional or even frankly eccentric. Those who are accustomed to flinging their arms around everyone they meet and those who solemnly shake hands will each view the other with puzzlement and alarm. On television we see men kissing one another on both cheeks in greeting and we may have come across it personally if we have travelled abroad. In parts of the Middle East it is strictly forbidden for a man even to sit on a seat in a public park next to a woman who is not his wife. And what do we make of the wild physical abandon with which goals or tries are met on the football and rugby fields in our own country? We each of us have cultural customs built deep into our nature and these can only be changed by a conscious effort on our part.

More importantly our own personal histories will affect the way we approach touching people. If we have come from a family where our parents kept their distance physically and rarely gave us a cuddle when we were small, we will find it that much harder to be free with our bear-hugs when we are adults. More dangerously, if we have been the victims of some kind of physical abuse in our childhood or youth, it would not be surprising if we grew up either with strong but only vaguely understood taboos about physical contact, or as people who keep making inappropriate demands. Often we do not fully realize where the inappropriate demands are coming from. Whatever our background, we need to be sensitive to differing past experiences, because it is all too easy to become exasperated with behaviour in our partner which jars with our own needs but in fact has its origin a long way back.

And the third factor about touching is that any display is always so ambivalent and so dependent upon mood. If, for example, somebody we do not know all that well gives us an enthusiastic hug, it might feel greatly life-enhancing, it might be just about OK, or it might feel quite threatening or even invasive. An observer will simply see a hug but the participants may have all kinds of emotions aroused in them, even differently in each participant. The subtleties about what people often call these days our own 'personal space' are often too unfathomable to work out in ourselves let alone in other people. Nevertheless, in spite of these hazards, the gift of touch can be wonderfully refreshing. For those who have lost through death a very long-term partner it is often the physical contact that is the most searing loss, as the bereaved poet Tennyson once put it in 'Break, break, break':
'Oh for the touch of a vanished hand
And the sound of a voice that is still.'

So this taking of our partner by the hand, a stroking of the cheek, a ruffling of the hair, a quick hug, an arm creeping round the shoulders, a kiss. These will be much the more valued when they are unexpected and unsought. Sometimes they may lead to bed, but much more often they are a simple expression of continuing love. However, do choose the right moment. An affectionate gesture will not often be welcome when our partner has his or her complete concentration elsewhere.

Now that I have written about how we can attain that unity of spirit by discovering intimacy, I shall continue in the next chapter to explain how intimacy is not threatened, but is enhanced, by the discovery of ourselves as separate people.

To do

Taking a Break

During the next four weeks see if you can plan a few hours one day when you and your partner can have some time together on your own. Then talk with him or her about the possibility of a night or two away during the next six months.

Remaining Separate People

It is great being in a warm, loving relationship. But every so often there is a bit of rebellion in the air. One voice within us says, 'I love loving and being loved'. Another voice says, 'Oh, do you now? It's all very well being married and having children and coping with families. It's all very well being a husband and a father, a wife and a mother, a couple, part of a household. But ... I want to be ME.' If you are passing through a rocky period in your relationship this second voice becomes rowdier. You probably will not have to look back very far to recall quarrels on these sorts of lines.

Now I believe it is right to want to be ME. I also believe that one of the main ways of discovering ME is when I become closely involved with other human beings. Sorting all this out—which I am attempting to do in this chapter—is no easy task. So I thought it might help if I invited you to try a 'To do' activity at the beginning of the chapter rather than at the end. It might concentrate all our minds.

To do
Activities together and alone
By filling in the boxes below, make lists of what you and your partner do separately and together.

Activities done with partner	Activities done by me alone	Activities done by partner alone

Then think about these questions:
● Would you like to change the position of any of the activities you have listed?
● If so, why?
● If you can, discuss the results with your partner.

You may have filled in activities to do with your job, child-rearing, housework, leisure, friendships, money, shopping and lots more. You may have discovered that you seem to do more than your partner, or the other way round, or that you would like to do rather more, or less, together than you do at the moment. What you will certainly have found is that there are both separate and joint spheres, and it would be surprising if you did not find yourself at least uneasy, and maybe positively resentful, about some of the things you have listed. 'How come she doesn't, or he doesn't, do this, that or the other?' or 'Why can't I ... or we... ?'

Such a reaction is perfectly normal. None of us effortlessly, or ever, reaches complete harmony on such subjects. Always there has to be compromise and the resolving of differences by means of negotiation, as we shall see in the next chapter.

Meanwhile I want first to talk of the importance of ourselves as individuals, then to explain how we grow as individuals in relationship to other people and finally to come back to some of the issues that your completion of the lists might have raised in your mind.

I Want to be Me

It is astonishing. There is nobody anywhere who is the same as you or me. Even identical twins, who emerge out of the same sac, can easily be distinguished by those who live alongside them. Each of us has different fingerprints and, we have discovered more recently, an original DNA print. The tiniest part of our bodies can be traced directly back to us.

Within Christian thinking this fact is often related to the opening chapters of the book of Genesis in the Bible, where the author attempts in story form to express the relationship between God and humankind. Having created the physical universe, God then sets about creating human beings. The author continues: 'So God created humankind in his image, in the image of God he created them; male and female he created them' (*Genesis 1.27*).

God's image in us makes us all recognizably God's handiwork but precisely not the same as one another because we are the products of his 'image'-ination. We are each of us a new creation distinct from every other creation. You may find this as heartwarming as I do. At least it makes a little more intelligible that other strand of Christian teaching that claims that God loves each of us individually. Loving people as one big lump of humanity makes very little sense even to us. Love needs to be expressed from person to person, as God's love is to us.

So our bodies are unique to us and our personalities, moulded as they are by our genes and our early influences, are also entirely original.

There are Things we Cannot Change

Alongside this lies a further truth about our existence as human beings. There are a considerable number of factors in our personality which we have no hope of changing. They are given. They are like ingredients in a store cupboard that we cannot replenish. It is out of those ingredients only that we have to make our life. Let us consider some of them.

- **Racial characteristics** We have no choice about the community we are born into, the colour of our skin, the religion of our parents or our national identity.

- **Family background** We cannot choose the parents who gave birth to us, their wealth or status, the jobs they do, the relatives they have or the number and sex of any brothers and sisters we may have.

- **Personal features** We cannot choose how tall or short we are, the facial features we were given at birth, the colour of our hair or the number of fingers and toes with which we were born.

- **Innate skills** We may or may not be naturally good at games, capable of reading for a degree, a possessor of a fine voice, a good musical ear or a talent for art, or skilled with our hands.

- **Our histories** Above all (and this is really quite hard to appreciate) we cannot alter in any way the facts and events that have happened in our past. That is to say, whatever has happened to us up to this very moment is a history personal to ourselves. Whether it is what people or events have or have not done to us, or what we have or have not done to ourselves, this history is now past and cannot be altered. As we have already seen, we can make use of our past decisively to alter what happens to us now, but the past itself is unchangeable.

That sounds and probably is daunting. Reading the list may make us wonder whether the whole of our life is determined for us. There is no doubt that many of us for some of the time, and some people for all of the time, become oppressed by the weight of a personal history. When we are feeling like this our cry is, 'If only...' If only I had different parents, a smaller nose, a sister, a reasonable singing voice, a religious faith, more money, a better start in life. And if only I had worked harder at school or had not tried to run away from home or had listened to my dad, who is dead now, or had gone to university. These sorts of feelings can easily lead to depression and even suicide.

We can Alter Things

We must take these feelings seriously because they are part of our existence as individuals. But that they are not the whole of our life can perhaps be seen by a brief look at a phrase you will be familiar with from your earliest days at school. 'Thy will be done,' says the Lord's Prayer and if you say it with an even voice, putting the same emphasis on each word as is usually the case, it becomes an act of resignation. God's will is unchangeable, so we must simply put up with it. Whatever will be, will be.

Now there must be an element in every religious life of accepting what God deals out to us, not least the factors I list above. There may also come times when a terminal illness, for example, might rightly bring a voluntary submission to whatever might happen to us. But I am much more inclined to believe that Jesus intended the phrase to sound rather different.

Suppose we say, 'Thy will be DONE' with an emphasis on the last word. That sounds like a summons. Seek the Will of God and then do it. Do not sit around waiting for things to happen to you. Take all the ingredients that have accumulated in your store cupboard and use them as the basis for the direction you choose to follow.

This is what makes that daunting list of factors we are not able to change less a burden to carry round with us than a summons to take responsibility for our lives. The ability to make choices is what distinguishes us as human beings. As individuals we can choose what job we shall do and whether we do it as well as we can or indifferently. We can choose who to marry, whether to have children and what sort of standards we shall apply in bringing them up. We can choose to take responsibility for other people in our lives—looking after a sick mother-in-law, managing a local boys' football team, treating our mates at work fairly. Even more importantly, we can choose to seek the truths about our own lives, to cast a cold eye on our faults and to admit them, to accept what our limits might be, to take risks and live with the consequences.

Choosing is never an easy option and we frequently become paralysed when we are faced with a multiplicity of choices or with one huge choice. And, truth to tell, there is rarely one completely obvious step to take. We usually have to listen to the best advice, consider the alternatives, make the choice and then work our way through whatever the outcomes might be.

So we are right to say, 'I want to be ME' because we rightly rejoice in being an individual absolutely unique in the world and, although there are many factors in our existence that we cannot change, we are also well-equipped to make significant innovations in the world about us. This element in our make-up is a remarkable gift. We must learn positively to encourage its development in one another and not to be afraid of it. It is indispensable to the formation of healthy relationships.

Becoming 'Me' Alongside Others

However, we cannot become ME entirely on our own. Our human condition is such that, although we are individuals, it is not possible for us to grow in our individuality except in relation to other individuals.

This is true obviously at the beginning of our lives. In the first few years of our existence we will not be able to survive at all unless somebody looks after us. In due course we grow away from this physical dependency but, as I have shown in earlier chapters, we remain closely attached to those who nurture, or fail to nurture, us. And this attachment, like our existence as separate individuals, is both inevitable and in principle a source of strength. Even our most personal choices are in some way a response to those who live about us. We need other people.

To take a sporting metaphor: if we have watched a golfer practising a swing on the driving range, we might have found something a little forlorn about him or her banging away hour after hour trying to get it exactly right. But if we learned that the golfer never, ever, played a game with anybody else we should think the behaviour frankly ludicrous. The point of improving one's skills is to compete successfully. However good the golfer becomes, the formula remains—no games, no sense.

So we exist not simply to develop ourselves but in order to form good relationships. At the same time we grow as individuals. I become ME, by means of the relationships I form and you become you through your relationship with me.

It is a sort of see-saw. For example, if at one time I have some sort of urgent internal concern on my hands I will be concentrating on myself as an individual (though I will be always wise to let trusted advisers inform my understanding). At other times my partner and I might be motoring rather well and will be occupied with our open enjoyment of other people's company (though here again being watchful lest we become too detached from our personal internal conditions). The see-saw can happen the other way round of course and become gravely damaging. I might on the one hand be so challenged by a relationship to a group or an individual that I cannot face it. So I retreat into a brooding silence which no amount of jollying along or irritated comment will drag me out of. I am now caught up inside myself in a harmful way. On the other hand I can throw myself frenziedly into whatever groups or relationships present themselves because it is too threatening to confront disturbing emotions which currently lie within.

It is not difficult to picture all those sorts of things happening in our marriages because, as I have said before, marriage exposes like no other relationship the heights and depths of who we are and what we might become.

In summary then, we can contribute to a fruitful marriage only when we ourselves are growing as individuals. At the same time our growth as individuals only takes place, in this context, when we are contributing to a fruitful marriage. The two factors—our growth as individuals and our contribution to the growth of others— intertwine and are dependent upon each other. We do not grow by trying to make ourselves like our partner. We grow by discovering ourselves in the working out of our partnership. An element of separateness therefore is vital to the stability of a mature partnership.

Practical Implications

With that understanding we are now ready to go back to the beginning of the chapter and to those boxes you may have filled in. What, in a practical way, are the implications of our being both separate individuals and committed for our development to other individuals, in particular our partner? How much should we try to be and to do together and how much apart?

Do not expect any binding directions. As original creations we can each expect to work out our own behaviour in our own way. But there are a few things to say which might ease your path.

Pursuing Separate Interests

We need to allow each other the freedom to pursue interests to which we have absolutely no desire to give any attention whatever. We can show a decent regard by enquiring how the activity went, e.g. 'Good game?' 'Many there?'

'See anyone we know?' but a well-ordered partnership should not need to pretend an interest that does not exist. As I have said, we are separate individuals, and though one might hope and even expect that a couple who decide to share their lives will have at least some common interests, it is unreasonable, and even alarming, to expect that they will work and play in total harmony.

There is not usually any trouble about this while the interests pursued by each partner are traditionally stereotyped. For instance, a man is expected to take an interest in sport or to wish to fiddle around with cars and their engines, while a woman takes a job simply to earn money and otherwise has a primary interest in domestic pursuits and keeping herself slim, fit and beautiful.

It is a little harder when, as happens more and more frequently, partners do not conform to these stereotypes and express a desire to differentiate themselves from their partner. One plays hockey or rugby and has a passionate interest in old French films while the other takes a ferocious interest in the garden and reads endless books about Napoleon. Nothing wrong with that, you may say, till one or the other becomes irritated at their partner's lack of interest or until baby-sitting problems arise when evening classes begin.

Curiously, it can be harder still when interests coincide. It sounds like a marriage much to be desired when a couple work alongside one another in blissful accord in the kitchen or in the garden. In practice many a woman flees from the kitchen as soon as a man enters it, and many gardens, through lack of an ability to agree about how a garden should be managed, are ultimately divided up into 'his' and 'her' sections.

Jealousies can easily arise where outside interests are concerned. One partner sits at home fantasizing about the other who is out at play. It is partly worry about who the partner might be meeting and what s/he might be getting up to, partly the fact that somebody has to be at home with the children and how come it so often happens to be me? Sometimes it can be about the very activity itself. It is the other partner, not you, who has the intelligence to read all those books and even write articles about Napoleon. It is the other partner who is strong enough to spend ninety minutes on a sports field when you would blow out in ten minutes, or who thinks nothing of going out for a drink with the women or men and arriving back an hour after the stated time. These are all matters for negotiation that I will address in the next chapter.

Meanwhile here is a fantasy of my own about a totally well-adjusted couple (which none of us is). She says, 'I'm off to a show tonight.' She adds she is going on her own. He does not feel the slightest sense of insult that he has not been invited. However, he changes his mind and says, 'I think I'll come too.' She replies, quite unfazed, 'That's great.' Alternatively she says to him, 'Would you like to come as well?' and he says, 'No, thanks,' at which she is not offended and goes anyway. We can all dream!

Being Apart

Some partnerships, where one partner is possibly a long-distance lorry driver, a sales rep, a night nurse, on the rigs or in the navy, have to survive quite long, regular absences. It is not easy to cope with. You can get used to a strange routine but it can be unsettling to find that the family has moved on in your absence and you were not part of that process. Many families, however, gain strength from the experience and make the most of it when the partner returns.

It is different if a partner chooses to go away for a few days, to visit friends or to deal with a family crisis. It can be lonely handling all the old problems on your own. And what if your partner is getting along absolutely fine without you, as you seem to hear when they speak to you on the phone? Or if you or your partner feels a rather greater sense of relief than appears to you to be justified? Absences like that can lead to wretched homecomings with underlying passionate needs for reassurance.

In truth healthy partnerships should thrive on short periods apart. Each has the opportunity to tap his or her own resources and discover fresh aspects of his/her self as an individual, while the partnership can gain from the chance to reflect upon how each relates to the other without the immediacy of constant companionship.

A more awkward sense of apartness is a characteristic of our present culture. It is when men and women plan to create and inhabit worlds where the opposite sex is not much welcome. Women complain that men at home are 'getting under our feet' as if men are somehow an alien presence there. Men in a mixed group breathe a collective sigh of relief when 'the women' leave them so that they can talk without restraint. Women live in worlds of mums' and toddlers' groups, coffee mornings and ladies' fashion. Men love sport, beer and a wide selection of men-only groups.

Of course, millions of people are not a bit like this but there can be inferences that people who do not conform to these stereotypes are in some way defective. Perhaps those who fall in with this pattern of behaviour might reflect upon what they are missing in the zest and understanding that are the gifts of the sexes working alongside one another.

Differing Viewpoints

E ach partner in a long-term relationship has come from a separate family. Those two families, like all families, have acquired habits and customs over the years, many of them inherited unthinkingly from previous families. They range from the completely unimportant (to most people), through rituals which have become second-nature to them, to deeply-held standards which the family strictly observe.

One family, for example, will regularly clean their shoes while the other, which nearly always wears trainers anyway, looks on in amazement. One family might always have tried to have one meal a day when the family sits down together and the children might have received careful instructions about how to handle a knife and fork. The other family rarely bothers. Members of that family take their meals when and where they can, informally. Or there are the standards that the children are taught concerning the level of respect that is due to the adults around them. For some families it is shocking for a child to question what an adult might say or demand. It is 'answering back'. Other families encourage free speaking on both sides and are not offended by it.

When two people start to live together they bring with them the traditions to which they have become accustomed. They are often quite unprepared to meet new traditions in their own backyard. They are protective of the customs they have brought with them to the marriage, astounded that somebody else can believe quite different things about how to live together, and can be made to feel intensely disloyal to their family of origin if they are invited to change their ways.

All these matters are the bread-and-butter of the daily discord in many families. Clashes can accumulate as if they are disagreements between the couple, whereas in fact the wrangling simply concerns the diversity of the families from which they have come. Parental visits can highlight the diversity and thereby give an opportunity to bring all the matters out into the open.

In the end obviously compromises have to be reached if a reasonably harmonious environment is to be created, and negotiation, or the resolving of differences, is the path towards that end. I now turn, therefore, to some possible strategies.

Dealing with Differences

Most of us find pictures and stories an easier way to grasp ideas than grappling with words alone, so through much of this chapter I shall use the story of an imaginary couple, Maggie and John, to help concentrate our minds.

John and Maggie have been married for nine years and have two children, Robert aged seven and Kate aged five. John, after a recent spell of unemployment, is now servicing computers locally for a national company on a three-year contract. Maggie worked part-time in a building society while her children were small but, now that they are both at school, she is back full-time. Her parents are five minutes down the road. John's father died when he was fourteen years old and his mother lives with her new husband one-and-a-half hours' drive away. It is suspected that Robert is dyslexic.

Large Issues Underlie Small Ones

In dealing with their differences there are two obvious initial truths that Maggie and John will need to come to terms with. The first is that, with scarcely ever an exception, larger issues underlie small ones. Always listen for the words, 'It's just a silly little thing' or 'Yeah, well, it's nothing really'. For example, they are all going to Sunday lunch with Maggie's parents. Maggie says that Robert ought to wear his best trousers because 'Mum will expect it'. John, who is looking forward to a chance to play football with Robert in the parents' larger garden, thinks it silly, nobody dresses up for lunch these days. Let the boy wear his jeans. They argue about it, with Robert furiously weighing in on his dad's side.

Now it is scarcely a matter of earth-shattering importance whether the lad wears jeans or his best trousers. And in the end one side of the argument prevails, or a compromise pair of trousers is agreed, and off they go, possibly muttering to themselves under their breath. It is in these mutterings that the larger issues reside. There might, for example, be an issue of manliness and therefore of the whole relationship between the sexes. John argues, 'You're making the boy into a cissy,' while Maggie responds, 'Well, look at the trouble you take with your appearance when YOU go out.' Models of being male or female are seriously important for developing young people, and both Maggie and John have been brought up with models carved out by their parents. The issue is far from being insignificant.

There is also the question of their family's relationship with the parents on each side. The culture, the ingrained habits of each of the families of origin, will not be the same. To concede to her parents' desire for some show of formality seems to Maggie the decent thing to do. John feels it is swanky and makes the whole day a misery for everybody. The parents just see a compliant daughter and a bad-tempered son-in-law. How two opposing cultures contrive a new working arrangement for the new family at the same time as they manage their previous families' ingrained customs is no easy task.

But perhaps the largest underlying issue is simply this: Who is going to win? Maggie or John? Winning is jeans for John and best trousers for Maggie. And who wins in this contest is an issue of power and authority. Does Maggie expect to win because she has taken charge of everything domestic and therefore sees John's plea as an impertinence? Does she always in fact expect everything at home to be carried out by all the members of the household, but only on her terms? And does John want to win because he fears losing authority in his own household and is very anxious to ensure that Robert, already fussed over because of his dyslexia, is not brought up as a 'mother's boy'? They will need to work out over the years whether they intend to separate power and authority, allocating areas in which the other does not interfere, or whether they keep learning the skills of sharing that same power and authority.

It seems amazing that all that could underlie what sort of trousers a little boy should wear, but so it does.

Never Completely Resolved

The other initial issue about differences I can deal with more shortly. It is to remind ourselves that resolving differences is not something that can be accomplished and then left behind us. It is more like climbing a hill in the Derbyshire Dales. We look up from the bottom and think, 'That's not so bad,' and we start climbing. Puffing, we reach the brow of the hill—and there it goes, on up again. We could not see from the bottom but there is another brow now to conquer. And so it goes on. We have made good progress, there is no doubt about that, and what we have climbed so far is a contribution towards the climbing of the whole of it. But in the matter of differences, although great strength comes from the mastering of each challenge, there will always be further high land ahead of us.

We shall need too to learn to distinguish between the differences that need to be resolved and those that have in the end either to be lived with or even, as we saw in the last chapter, welcomed as a vivid sign of each partner's identity. Ahead of the event we cannot predict into which category this particular difference will fall. Indeed it is often only in the tackling of the difference that it becomes plain what sort of dispute is in hand.

So, for example, Maggie, after a year back in full-time work, is unexpectedly offered the management of her building society branch in a town fifty miles away. All hell breaks loose back at home. Maggie, although thrilled at the confidence expressed in her, is not quite sure whether she is thrilled enough to face all the hassle of travelling to work or perhaps moving house, of leaving her parents, of child-care problems and of now earning more than John. John, pleased for Maggie, is nevertheless resolutely determined to avoid a wholesale alteration in his daily routine and a shift of power in Maggie's favour. Because he recognizes that those are both self-interested reasons for arguing against the move, he pleads a case where he knows Maggie will be vulnerable and says that the children cannot be put at risk in this way.

Somewhere along the line Maggie and John will discover whether Maggie's development as an individual is or is not worth fighting for.

So do not expect everything to be resolved or even resolvable, and do remember that the small interchanges of everyday life most often conceal and, if attended to, also reveal, the larger issues that really govern our lives.

To do

A Big Row

The next thing I want to do is to give you an example of a big row between Maggie and John. Please think about how you would begin to tackle the row and then see how far my suggestions, which follow, match those that you have come up with. Here's the row, which seems at one level to be to do with sex but, there again, there are a whole lot of other concerns aroused as well. It is one of those gruelling rows which, the longer it goes on, the harder it becomes to recall whatever it was all about in the first place.

Relationships are just getting sourer. There are sharp exchanges—'Do you mind …?' 'Look, I'm busy' 'What! You've spent the lot?' 'I don't know when I'll be back' and so on. Otherwise barely a civil word. The children tiptoe around uneasily. John's unexplained absences are part of the trouble. Maggie suspects he is having an affair down at the Leisure Centre. In fact he is not, but he stays out late to punish her. Let her stew! He implies she is frigid. Nobody mentions that he is sometimes impotent. They make love angrily or not at all.

How did it begin? An argument about bringing up the children? Mother-in-law trouble? One partner's extravagance or meanness? A disastrous holiday? It is hard to remember now. The whole family feels miserable.

Perhaps you would like to pause at this point and think your way into John and

Maggie's position. What do you think it might feel like to be where they are? And then ask yourself: precisely what action would you take to begin to mend the relationship?

....

....

Some Suggestions

I shall now put forward a few suggestions of my own. These are bound to come out in rather an ordered fashion as if to say, 'Follow this formula and all will be well'. It will not, I fear. Human relationships are not that uncomplicated. All I can do is to offer some possible ways forward that many people over the years have found helpful, and to invite you to try them out with your partner. The order does not much matter—we tend to come into such discussions at different points—but there is a certain logic in following this outline.

Breaking the Ice

This may be the hardest bit for John and Maggie because neither has any idea how any approach at all will be received and they will be frightened of what might happen. They will invent in their heads all kinds of scenarios for not doing so, e.g. 'If I say anything he is bound to fly off the handle and...', 'I've only got to raise an eyebrow and Maggie goes off into a sulk for days...' Nevertheless the misery will continue unless one or the other of them dares to break the ice.

It might be too difficult to begin talking face-to-face, once the decision has been made, and some couples start by using the telephone or the pen. So Maggie might ring John at work and say, 'Look, I'm sorry. Let's talk' or John might put the same message on a note on her side of the bed. Sometimes it can be even simpler than that, a gesture or a touch when all the signs seem propitious. I do not think this is ducking the issue. It is exceedingly tough to begin negotiations especially when, as in John and Maggie's case, their recent history together is so muddled and so depressing. The fatal mistake for them to make is to suppose that when the word 'sorry' has been mentioned, then the whole episode can be forgotten. 'Sorry' is only the very beginning, the way into harmony and not the achieving of it.

And perhaps it might be as well at this point to say a word or two about 'sorry' and forgiveness and reconciliation. There is absolutely no doubt that Jesus demanded an extremely high standard of reconciliation. He told St Peter, who thought that he would be doing wonderfully well if he forgave somebody seven times, that seventy times seven was more like it. In other words his disciples must NEVER fail to forgive. But what he also went on to say was that forgiveness has to be mutual. 'Forgive us our sins as we forgive those who sin against us.' He told the story of the servant who owed a fortune to his master but, at his earnest request, was let off the debt. The servant went out and found a fellow-servant who owed him a pound or two and, because the poor fellow could not pay, had him thrown into gaol. Jesus' verdict was, 'You wicked servant!' Read the story in Matthew 18.21–35.

Now the relevance of this to John and Maggie's row is that when either of them says 'sorry' the other will immediately be tempted to say, 'I should think so too!' In other words the person to whom 'sorry' is said at once takes a lofty position from which he or she can look down on the partner. Instantly the partner is infuriated both because the other is taking the moral high ground and because it is untrue that the fault lies only on one side.

The truth is that there is never, ever, an occasion in a relationship where the fault lies with just one partner, and this for the simple reason that the fault is in the relationship. Grasp this: that Maggie and John have a faulty relationship, rather than seeking faults in either of them—and suddenly we perceive forgiveness as a rich gift, offered to both of them equally and to be received with humility.

It begins with 'sorry' or some similar gesture of reconciliation but cannot end there because their journey of discovery out of the trouble they have landed up in has only just started. This leads therefore to the next stage.

Claiming Time

Once the ice has been broken, it is essential to find time to discuss the issues involved. And time, naturally, is the one thing that both Maggie and John say they have not got. It is true too. For one couple to handle at the same time two full-time jobs, looking after the children, cooking and housework, taking trouble with ageing parents and fulfilling some responsibility to the community, e.g. school sports days, the occasional fête, going to church, is extremely hard work and can be very exhausting.

More exhausting, however, is to bear that burden at the same time as they have a rotten relationship. Few things pull us down more and lead to a stressful life than an inability to live comfortably alongside our partner. Energy spent in fighting or in glum withdrawal is energy wasted. To be rid of it frees us for more positive tasks and actually releases new sources of zest and vigour.

So Maggie and John need to negotiate some time alone with each other. It might be possible to go out for a meal together but experience shows that there are often too many distractions and too much noise in a pub or a restaurant. They need to give one another enough sharp-eyed attention to pick up the nuances of what each of them says, and they cannot do that if one of them, just at the crucial moment of course, keeps tripping off to the bar for the next half-pint of lager. It is better to dump the children on the in-laws and either go off into the park or stay at home and switch off the phone.

I call it 'claiming' time because either Maggie or John can be hesitant about asking a hard-working partner to disturb a well-practised routine. It feels selfish, but in fact it is merely responsible. There are few ways other than discussion for the resolving of differences.

Stating their Case

So here are Maggie and John sitting in the park watching the ducks. What does either of them say that does not simply go round in circles, dragging up all the sins and misdemeanours of the past and leaving them at the end of the day feeling worse than ever?

A strategy which is often helpful is for each partner to allow the other to speak, however hesitantly, without interruption, or anyway with as little interruption as the other partner can manage. It comes back to the issue I raised in an earlier chapter about listening. When we listen, for much of the time we tend to hear the other person through a sort of gauze curtain that is the accumulation of all our resentments over the months and years. Instead of listening to the other person, we listen through our own experiences and thus fail to hear anything new. To listen to 'the music of the words' we have to make the effort to tear aside this gauze curtain and to enter into the feelings and experiences of the other. One of the simplest ways of doing this is to stop talking ourselves and just to listen.

The trouble about that is that we fall to self-justification at the drop of a hat. Eric Berne, in a famous book called *Games People Play*, talks about one game which he entitles, 'Yes, but…' In this psychological game an individual listens superficially to the other person and at the earliest possible opportunity negates all that he or she has heard with a statement of its opposite. 'Yes, that's all OK, but… ' The individual has not really heard but is simply waiting impatiently for a pause into which to put his or her own side of the argument. It does not take much reflection to recall ourselves playing that game. If John and Maggie play the 'Yes, but…' game they will undoubtedly end the day in further recriminations.

But if they listen to one another carefully it will not be long before the discussion becomes a painful one. For the fact is that organizing a shift in the relationship implies that each partner is in for some changes, and any change in behaviour is desperately hard to confront. Yet Maggie and John will need to recognize that they have only two choices before them: either to face the pain of change or to live with the pain of staying where they are. It is a painful choice either way but only the first can help them to grow.

Making Some Agreement

The world of human relationships is full of the temptation to take short cuts and one of the most common at this point is for Maggie or John or both of them to make a series of grand, and probably rather woolly, promises. He says, 'I will turn over a completely new leaf,' or 'I will never be late back from the Leisure Centre again.' She says, 'From now on I won't spoil Robert, even though he is dyslexic,' or 'I won't ask you for any more housekeeping.' He says, 'I won't run down your parents.' She replies, 'And I won't nag you about finding a better-paid job.'

So the Kingdom of Heaven has arrived? I am afraid not. People do not change that quickly. The intentions are excellent but over the next few weeks all such statements are likely to go the way of most New Year resolutions. Our hopes are stronger than our capacity for carrying them into effect.

The secret in negotiation between couples is to avoid resolutions of any kind. That may sound as if I am denying any place for the human will in our lives. Surely you are not saying, you might argue, that it is impossible for people to make decisions and to stick with them? Far from it. There might well be areas in your life, take giving up smoking for example, where you have said, 'This I am going to do' and you have stuck to it. Obviously this is admirable and although it is so difficult, most of us, in one area or another, have had a shot at it.

But I do not believe that the language of resolution, which is an individual language, is the right one to use in a conversation between couples. Where partners are negotiating it is far healthier to think in terms of agreements—that is, statement of further intention which is clear, specific, moderately short-term and achievable.

Thus, for example, John and Maggie might agree as a first step that next week John will come back from the Leisure Centre early enough for Maggie to go and get her hair done. They also agree that Maggie will make an appointment with the school so that they can both go and talk to the form teacher about Robert's possible dyslexia. In the slightly longer term they agree that at least twice this month they will leave the late-night ironing and video and get to bed with some energy left to try to renew their love-making.

Not front-page news, but it does not need to be. All that has happened is that they have begun a new journey, or rather taken up the old one again. The agreements are clear, specific and easily achievable. At the end of next week, all being well, Maggie will have had her hair done and Robert will have his appointment fixed. At the end of the month they will have had a couple of sessions in bed and begun again to discover how much they still have to learn about love-making. If they do succeed in fulfilling these agreements, or at least some of them, soon there is a more stable plateau from which they can begin the next stage of the journey. At the same time they can expect there to be a softening of the atmosphere. A spirit of co-operation, rather than antagonism, begins to emerge. To have achieved even one of the agreements reached is in itself a strengthening of the marriage.

After such a conversation it can be valuable to agree as well that they will take some time together again in a month or so in order to review how far their undertakings have been fulfilled—and, if they feel good about it, to make a few more.

Children

There are other books available that deal specifically with child-rearing. If you would like some help with parenting issues, they might be the place to look. I want to talk a bit about children not in order to go over that sort of ground but rather to discuss the effect of children on the relationship. The bond that holds a couple together changes radically when a child is born. The question is, what sort of changes are we talking about?

And the first thing to say is that, as you may have discovered already, it is one of the most intensely exciting events of our lifetimes. To be presented with a tiny infant, totally dependent upon you and for whose wellbeing you have the entire responsibility, is an awe-inspiring experience. Fergal Keane, the BBC correspondent, expressed something of that wonder in a piece he wrote a few years ago on the birth of his first child, Daniel.

'My dear son, it is six o'clock in the morning on the island of Hong Kong. You are asleep cradled in my left arm and I am learning the art of one-handed typing. Your mother, more tired yet more happy than I've ever known her, is sound asleep in the room next door and there is soft quiet in the apartment … Your coming has turned me upside down and inside out. So much that seemed essential to me has, in the past few days, taken on a different colour … In a world of insecurity and ambition and ego, it's easy to be drawn in, to take chances with our lives, to believe that what we do and what people say about us is reason enough to gamble with death. Now, looking at your sleeping face, inches away from me, listening to your occasional sigh and gurgle, I wonder how I could have ever thought glory and prizes and praise sweeter than life.'

Keane F, *Letter to Daniel: Despatches from the Heart* (BBC Publications, 1996)

The other thing to say is that, in the same way as a child turns your emotional life upside-down, so does he or she bring practical turmoil into a household. Everything has now to be accommodated to this little mite. You used to be able to go out in the evening, to visit the shops, to make love, to take off for holidays just whenever your work-routine permitted it. Now you cannot do so. You used to enjoy your job and your job prospects, but now both are a little uncertain. You are tied night and day by the presence of a third person whose demands are expressed very vocally but in such an invariable way that you are frightened you are missing something. You tiptoe around the sleeping form at night, listening for the signs of regular breathing.

Over time your fears subside but other problems emerge. The very first of these may be that on the contrary the experience of childbirth has never come your way and you are desperate that it should. Childlessness can have a profound effect upon a marriage.

Childlessness

Those who bring children into the world without trouble sometimes have difficulty in appreciating how hard it is for couples who want to have a child but it does not seem to happen. Not to be able to have a child can be a bitter and heart-breaking experience, particularly for women, who are much closer than men to the process of creation. Such a person sees all her friends glowing with the health of pregnancy and chattering to one another about methods of feeding, while she can scarcely bear to look into a pram and utter words of encouragement to the proud new mother. This helplessness can create barriers between a couple.

Pam, for example, has been married for eight years and there is still no sign of a child. She and her husband have been to the doctor, gone through all the appropriate tests, and there does not seem to be any physical cause. They have even contemplated IVF treatment but have been unable to find a NHS hospital that offers the service.

They are not the sort of couple that talks easily to one another. Pam is not sure that her husband understands how painful it is for her. He becomes irritated if she talks about it too much. 'Oh, do stop going on about it,' he complains. 'You know we're doing everything we can. We just have to wait and see, that's all.' Pam believes that he is upset but will not let it show, so she feels constrained to draw in her horns too. She nurses her own misery when she is alone.

She has two fears about her husband though. The first is that he might not be as upset as she is. She fears that secretly he might not welcome the curtailment of his freedom that a child would bring. If he felt like that she would be very angry. On the other hand she fears that he might alternatively be extremely unhappy about not having a child, and if he were to express that she is not sure she could bear a doubling of her anguish. Both fears stop her talking to him about it.

What she does is to resolve her frustration by being bright and cheerful with everybody except him. With him she is snappy and offhand because her unhappiness has to have an outlet somewhere and he seems to be the safest recipient of it. (She may very well be wrong about that.) It is not that she in the least blames him for her childlessness. She would be horrified to be accused of that. But her emotions are like a spring bubbling out of the earth. If she tries to build a house over the spring to stop the water coming, nothing happens except that the water either undermines the foundations of the new building and it collapses or the water is diverted and springs up somewhere else. Pam's emotions cannot ultimately be entirely suppressed, and it is her husband who is the safety valve for her.

What is likely to happen now is that Pam and her husband will get in a muddle about the sort of direction their marriage is taking. This might particularly display itself in bed when love-making might begin to lose some of its joyful spontaneity and become hopelessly subject to temperature-taking and the monthly cycle. The childlessness becomes a huge rock in the path of life and all journeys stop until it has either been removed or a way round the rock is discovered. And if it eventually becomes clear that the couple is never likely to have children they will need to reassess their future.

God has always intended that love should be shared in ever-widening circles. If Pam and her husband are not to be given the opportunity of learning, through the gift of children, how to share their life more widely, then they will have to find other ways of enlarging their marriage. The temptation will be for them to go their separate ways and find comfort in the company of members of their own sex, Pam maybe back with her mother, and her husband down at the pub. The exciting thing to do is to seek new paths together. Couples who do not have the responsibilities that children bring can be tremendously valuable to their community and can often find ways of contributing their skills and their care to young people through school and leisure activities. Thousands of ill-parented children are crying out for it.

The First Child

Couples are nearly always enchanted with their first-born. Yet, however devoted they are to one another and to their new child, it remains true that two people are now three people. What they have been learning in the first years of their marriage is how to deepen their love for one another. What they each of them now have to learn is how to share their love with two people who, in their different ways, demand and offer love of their own.

What they will quickly learn is the reality of jealousy. Contrary to what you might have been taught in Sunday School I do not believe this to be often a massive sin. Jealousy is simply the natural consequence of having to share our love around. It becomes sinful only when we allow it to dominate us, that is, when we refuse to accept that those we love will also love other people.

Let us take Brian this time. He has been married for four years. His wife has just had a baby. He was present at the birth and he is pleased that she has decided not to go back to work for the time being. They have had a really fruitful relationship up to now and they have both looked forward to the child's birth.

However, although he does not say much, Brian is finding himself oddly resentful. He quite recognizes that his wife, who is sensitive to such things, is going out of her way to show that she still loves him. Yet he senses somehow that, whatever she says or does for him, she has acquired a sort of 'inward eye' which is perpetually turned elsewhere. The baby is demanding a massive amount of attention not only in physical terms (and he will be glad when the child sleeps through the night at least) but in the claims it makes on his wife's devotion. He loves his wife, he loves the new baby, he even finds, in a sense that he does not in the least understand, that the whole business is mixed up with the loss of his Mum. But he still feels rejected, pushed out of a charmed circle which is not designed for men.

The trouble is that he has had a fairly bleak period recently where sex is concerned. Even where sex has been possible his wife has not shown much enthusiasm (that 'inward eye' again). It does not help, and he is a bit embarrassed about this, that it makes him feel randy whenever he sees his wife breast-feeding.

This is all far too difficult to talk about. He does not have the words even when he catches glimpses of what the experience might be about. He therefore retreats into a silence, which, if she is not particularly understanding, can lead his wife to believe that he is losing his love for her. She is alarmed but at the moment may not have the energy to do much about it.

At this point I believe one of the factors we have to come to terms with is that men often find the world of feelings much harder to handle than women do. There is a sort of emotional incoherence in many men which neither they nor their partners can fathom. If Pam in the last section built a house over the spring of her emotions, many men have built a massive tower-block over theirs. Probably it has much to do with early conditioning—'Big boys don't cry' and so on—that is repeated in generation after generation. This lack of emotional maturity can produce an aching loneliness in some men that is barely concealed by an outward display of confidence.

You will of course recognize the last paragraph as something of a wild generalization. There are many, many wonderful exceptions to it. But if it rings any bells with you it might help, if you are a woman, to take that little more trouble to penetrate a man's outer skin. If you are a man, it might help to reconcile yourself to your own personal history and to consider where you would like to move from here.

Rearing Children

The first child does not have to be more than a few weeks old before couples face potential conflicts over child-rearing practices. Take feeding, for example. A wife has been brought up with the belief, or has acquired the belief through her friends outside the home, that babies should be fed on demand. So, desperate as she is to be a really good mother for the child, whenever the baby so much as whimpers at any time of the day or night, she downs tools and feeds it at once.

Her husband feels that to respond to a child's every demand might get him or her into the way of thinking, as he or she grows up, that the world will always be like that. The child's demands are always going to be met immediately and without question. He feels that his wife is making a rod for her own back. She is exhausted enough as it is with all the broken nights. Secretly he is pretty angry that all this attention is being lavished on the child and precious little comes his way.

In such a situation—or the reverse of it, where the wife thinks it is healthy to 'let the child cry a bit' and he feels she is being cruel and hard-hearted—it is usually the woman's will that prevails. After all, she is nearly always the child's main provider in the early months and years.

Very prominent between the couple at this stage are the couple's parents. They may not live near by or even, sometimes, have much interest in their new grandchild, but their influence in the new family will be strong. The forceful arguments of wife or husband concerning feeding, to take that as an example, may be either in conformity with or in defiance of their own parents' practices. Either way the arguments, and at times the very voices, of the families of origin will be heard again in the new family. 'You're just like your mother/father,' is often said and is not infrequently true.

Later on in the child's life, when his or her father is not quite so out of his depth as he was when the child was an infant, discussions about how children should be brought up become more even-handed though still complex. So often they revolve around the sort of standards of behaviour that should be expected of a child and what parents should do to enforce those standards. Examples are not hard to find.

- What time should they go to bed and how often should they be allowed to stay up to watch a special TV programme?

- At what age, if at all, should they be allowed to walk to school on their own?

- What level of privacy should they be permitted? If they have their own bedroom, do you knock before you go in?

- How much help in the house should they be encouraged to offer?

- Is fourteen years old too young for them to baby-sit their younger brothers and sisters?

- Do you smack them and, if not, what punishment do you have up your sleeve?

- What level of 'respect' do you demand?

In many of these cases couples will be struggling with reconciling the customs and practices of the two families they come from. One family used to do this and one did that, so what do we do now? It becomes even more involved if the parents additionally come from mixed backgrounds. It is simple to imagine the further complications that might arise if partners come from different church backgrounds, e.g. liberal and conservative evangelical, or if they have parents of different races, or if one family of origin is sports-loving and outdoor and the other loves the theatre and books.

When they reach their teenage years, children will often compel their parents into an alliance because they begin to bring back from their peers at school quite novel ideas about how they should live their lives. Parents, wrong-footed and baffled, may turn to one another for sanctuary. At least the old battlegrounds are familiar.

The clue in dealing with all this is, of course, to keep talking. Talk to one another, to other parents who will be facing exactly the same problems as you are, to your parents on both sides. Your parents especially might sometimes have been baffled by the directions that you took and could have wisdom of their own if they are prepared to share it. But the most important people of all to talk to are the children themselves. For all their bravado, they too are facing brand new challenges every day of their lives. Learning the habit of open honesty with them can be dramatically rewarding.

An Encouraging Tale

L et me end with a true-life story that demonstrates how quite modest understandings about human relationships can bring about significant improvements in family life. It comes from a short video in Michael Quinn's parenting material and is designed to show how extreme misbehaviour in quite small children can be totally altered by practising a few simple principles.

We first see a highly embarrassed young couple contemplating their son, aged about five, kicking and screaming on the floor of a supermarket. The boy is quite out of control and whatever the parents do only seems to make him worse. They talk to him and he screams some more; they take his arm and he jerks back on to the floor again. So the boy and his family are taken to a family centre where they are offered eight sessions over a course of weeks. We are shown a room with lots of toys where the boy and his father are invited to play. Two therapists observe from behind a two-way mirror, invisible to the boy and his father. The father has an ear-piece in his ear so that the therapists can talk to him quietly without the boy being aware of it.

The first thing that the boy does is to look around in fury, to make for the door and to charge off down the corridor. The therapists patiently invite the father to go after him and bring him back. The father is then to stand with his back to the door, preventing the boy from leaving again. He is advised to say and do nothing except stand there. The boy beats everything with his fists and races round the room bent on destruction. The father again is advised to say and do nothing save to prevent damage to the boy and his surroundings. The boy looks up at his father after a time, nonplussed.

Here we have the first two simple principles at work:
1. Create reasonable boundaries in which the child can feel safe—so, stand at the door to prevent him going out and see that nothing is destroyed.

2. Do not reinforce bad behaviour by paying attention to it—so, as long as the boy rants and raves, peacefully ignore it all and, after a time, draw his attention to other more interesting things to do.

The boy in due course begins to play with some toys and the father, through his ear-piece, is encouraged to sit alongside him and, as he plays, gently start describing what the boy is doing. 'Oh, I see. You're trying to make an engine. Now you're picking up that piece—I wonder where you're going to put that.' After a few minutes of this the boy looks round with wonderment and, in a moment of pure delight, he goes up to his father, puts his arms around his neck and hugs him.

So we reach the third simple principle, which is:
3. Give the boy some attention when he is least expecting it—so, be alongside the boy as he plays, and demonstrate your interest without interference.

At the end of the video we see the boy walking hand-in-hand with his mother and father, as normal as anyone could wish.

Most parents over the years experience many such moments of fulfilment and joy.

To do

Parenting Support

Bring several parents together with you and your partner to explore some parenting issues. There are resources that you can use including those produced by Michael Quinn's Family Caring Trust that provides material for parents of *The Noughts to Sixes*, *The Fives to Fifteens*, and *Parenting Teenagers* as well as programmes on parental assertiveness and *Parenting and Sex*. In addition it is well worth using The Family Caring Trust's adult materials. There are four weekly sessions for groups of women without their partners called *Growing in Love* and six weekly sessions for committed couples at all stages called *Couple Alive*. Further information can be obtained from:
The Family Caring Trust,
8 Ashtree Enterprise Park,
Newry,
Co. Down,
BT34 1BY
Telephone: 01693-64174

Telephone Help Line

In 1999 the Government provided finance to enable the establishment of a national telephone help line for parents called PARENTLINE. The telephone number is 0808 800 2222. So if you want to talk about a parenting issue, use that number.

Money and Jobs

All of us face so many issues about money and jobs that it is difficult to know where to begin. With respect to money we can ask ourselves: Who does the money I earn belong to—me or the family? Who pays the mortgage? Who pays the household bills and out of whose money? Who handles all the money and does it demean the man if it is his wife? What are our feelings about overdrafts, credit cards, debt and savings? What happens if one partner is a spendthrift and the other is not? How does one partner enforce sensible behaviour in the other? Do we keep accurate accounts or just enough to satisfy the Inland Revenue? If we have only one car, who does it belong to and who has the first use of it?

There are just as many questions to resolve about jobs: If both partners work, whose job comes first? For example: if the children are ill, who stays home from work? What happens if one partner gets promotion and it looks as if the family will have to move house? (See John and Maggie a couple of chapters ago.) Or do the partners live apart during the week? Can the husband bear it if his wife earns more than he does? Who meets the children from school? How much does the woman expect her partner to take a share in the housework (and no, that is not a sexist question because, apart from house husbands, how many husbands do you know that invite their wives to help with the housework)? Suppose one partner for excellent reasons does not wish to work, or for not-so-good reasons is work-shy, what should the other partner do about it? What are the relative merits of full-time and part-time work?

Considering all such questions I came to the conclusion that the most helpful thing I can do is to suggest three standpoints from which the issues can be considered. These standpoints are:

- Mutual trust is at the heart of all successful relationships.

- Reliable care for the children of the family is of the very first importance, particularly when they are small.

- The ordering of priorities in our family life is a critical, but continually shifting, debate.

These standpoints are broad enough to be applicable to many aspects of a married partnership. Here I shall use them first to talk largely but not exclusively about money, secondly to address issues of how jobs affect child care, and thirdly to range more widely over marital priorities.

Trusting one Another

All of us in partnerships have made an act of commitment of some kind that had at the heart of it an implication that our future partner was to be trusted. Thereafter the trust has to be tested in the fire of everyday living. Our relationship thrives or expires on our trust in each other or its absence. It grows over the years as we discover each other, in small and greater matters, to be trustworthy.

The first principle in trust is a preparedness to turn our back on secrets and to be as open and honest as, in the circumstances, it is possible to be. Secrets in a family can be very damaging and can be passed down stubbornly from one generation to the next. When all parties on each side of a secret are treading warily around each other, not saying what they mean to say and cutting short their sentences meaningfully, or angrily trying to decipher hidden messages behind ambivalent statements, trust goes out of the window. What comes in is suspicion, fear, misinformation, acrimony and separateness.

Of course there are parts of our experience which are so painful that we rightly take extreme care with whom we share them or whether we do so at all, even with our spouse for the time. But our instinct all the time needs to be on the side of disclosure. On this principle therefore our handling of money could take the following form.

A Free Exchange of Information

Few things destroy trust more certainly than a decision by one partner to withhold information from the other about the state of their finances. It is not difficult to do this. One partner may get into the habit of slipping a couple of notes from his or her pay packet into a pocket or bag. A small legacy is not disclosed or is only half disclosed. One partner saves on the housekeeping and begins to build up a private account. Information about an increase in salary is concealed. On the other hand one partner may be getting into financial difficulties and may go to extravagant lengths to hide it, sometimes spending the more wildly, at other times enforcing grotesque economies in order to disguise the true position.

Underlying such strategies may be some disturbing feelings of insecurity. Money is a very powerful commodity not simply for the goods it can buy but also as a defence against the vulnerabilities we prefer not to address directly. Having money, or pretending that we have it, makes us feel good. It wins friends. It shows the world that we are somebody to be reckoned with. It demonstrates to our partner that we are strong and reliable. And it does this in a manner which is not to be gainsaid, with notes flashed around and new purchases to be admired. This is not an advantage lightly to be discarded even when, as the family grows and one partner perhaps stops working, money becomes tighter.

Understanding such sensitivities should prevent us making too many frontal attacks on our partner based upon credible suspicions or evidence. Barking accusations rarely leads to an agreed resolution. On the other hand it is fatal to turn a blind eye to what you think might be going on because that slowly erodes the trust that is an essential part of building up a relationship. Sharing your anxieties and difficulties about money, possibly recounting some of your personal history with it, can be a way into a discussion that can lead to a fruitful outcome.

Codes of Behaviour

Methods of handling money bring out the strongest convictions in people. Some are carefree. A proportion of these will spend lavishly, live permanently with an overdraft, are entirely unworried about being in debt and pay bills only when they arrive in red ink. Another group of the carefree keep their accounts on the stub of their chequebook, hand out pocket money to the children liberally and have no special principles, save to avoid spending more than they have.

Those who are more disciplined about money often view the carefree with some alarm. They cannot imagine how it is possible to live without knowing exactly where every penny goes. Some of these are fearful of money. Perhaps they have been brought up in a house where a father, extravagant with his money, has left the rest of the family in real deprivation. Whatever the cause, a parsimonious streak has taken root and money becomes an enemy which has to be ruthlessly besieged day by day. Others, not in the least oppressed by money, need nevertheless to be in complete control of their finances and maintain precise accounts of income and expenditure.

It is not difficult to imagine what might happen in a marriage if the carefree meets the parsimonious.

My view is that it does not really matter how a couple handle their finances provided that they come to some agreement about it and stick to it. Inland Revenue requirements will ensure that most of us have to keep a basic minimum of financial records, but for the rest it is a matter of choice, habit and consensus. We all use different methods—pots on the mantelpiece for the different monthly or quarterly bills, a running balance for household expenditure, using or not using credit and debit cards, keeping accounts or good enough figures on chequebook stubs. Once we have agreed them we need only to ensure that the terms of the arrangements are renegotiated when circumstances change as, for example, if one partner moves from full-time to part-time work.

The pitfall in all this is debt. Most of us will have a debt on our house in the form of a mortgage and will be unable to finance the purchase of a car without some kind of loan. Beyond those two items the acquisition of further debt can be hazardous. It is easy to advocate caution, not so easy to advise one partner what to do if the other is foolhardy. Slippage is the commonest problem. 'Oh, well. We really need this item, but we won't have any more...' As the credit card debt rises it becomes more and more difficult to finance the loan.

Early action is the only reliable advice. A £500 debt is easier to manage than one of £5,000. We should not be afraid to take advice, from friends or family more experienced than we are or from bodies like the Citizens' Advice Bureau which has a high expertise on debt.

Generosity

Finally, where money is concerned, Christians have to face some pretty brutal comments from the Bible. For example: 'Those who want to be rich fall into temptation and are trapped by many senseless and harmful desires that plunge people into ruin and destruction' (*1 Timothy 6.9*).

We do not have to look far around us today to discover that sort of story still going on. Money is a wonderful friend but a powerful enemy. One of the ways of taming it is by means of generosity.

It is a tonic to give one another carefully chosen presents, not just at birthdays and Christmas but sometimes out of the blue and as an act of sheer love. Generosity, like covetousness, feeds on itself. Soon the calls on our love from outside the house, or even our country, make themselves heard. We start to enjoy managing our responsibilities towards our parents, our children, our church and our struggling neighbours. It is immensely rewarding. As Jesus so warmingly puts it, 'The measure you give will be the measure you get back' (*Luke 6.38*).

Reliable Care for the Child

The number of full-time jobs in Britain has fallen from twenty-one million in 1955 to nineteen million in 1995. However this does not seem to have prevented women from finding full-time jobs today in greater numbers than they did in the 1950s. This is probably due to what is sometimes called the 'feminization' of the workplace in the sense that many more available full-time jobs these days, in an increasingly technological world, can be undertaken equally well by men and women.

Before the arrival of children it is usual for both men and women to be out at full-time work. As soon as a woman falls pregnant, anxieties begin. Some new mothers, often those with responsible and fulfilling careers, are determined that they will take the time out for the birth of their baby that the law permits and then, having arranged child care for the baby, return immediately to full-time work. Yet this is a much smaller proportion of women than newspaper articles might lead us to believe. A recent survey, quoted by Oliver James in *Britain on the Couch,* showed that only eleven per cent of women in Britain with a child under one year old were in full-time work and that the figure had crept up to a mere thirteen per cent when their child was under three years old. The vast majority of women with a very young child do not work full-time.

But a little more than half of them do of course work part-time and I imagine it is into this part-time job market that the Government is attempting to encourage single mothers.

Why do mothers work at all? There are a whole variety of reasons that do not at the moment show any general trend. Some mothers love their work and long to return. Some do not much enjoy it but frankly they need the money. Paying the mortgage and keeping a family on only one pay packet when they have been used to two is just too much for the household purse to manage. Others do not always need the money but cannot face solitary days at home with only a baby for company. Others again would like to work but cannot obtain a sufficiently high-paying job to pay for child care. And there are also women who believe that men take full advantage of the fact that a woman will normally become entangled in child-birth issues in order to corner all the best jobs and keep women in their place.

Whichever, or however many, of those categories you fall into, there can be no question that in the vast majority of cases a heavy responsibility falls on the woman for child care. It is the woman who is most often torn between the child and the workplace, and it is the man who has to strive to put himself emotionally in his partner's shoes. For, whatever their ultimate decisions about who shall stay at home and when, the over-riding concern for the couple needs to be a friendly, reliable and unbroken source of care for the child.

Every competent authority agrees that nothing is more important for the child than a consistency of care. His or her development into a mature, integrated human being may depend upon the absolute security he or she has found in his or her young childhood. The mother herself, or the father, is the best source of care (which brings bewitching enjoyments to the parent), but a benevolent grandparent, a warm-hearted neighbour or a well-vetted child-care professional can be a satisfactory substitute.

Whether or not a couple accepts this priority, as parents they are always going to be faced with a series of painful decisions about jobs. In a family where each partner is bent upon a serious career, key moments arise when a choice has to be made between the relative importance of the two careers. To be honest, there are not many men who, when their partner has the opportunity to progress, will take the lesser job in order to accommodate her. In a family where there is a full-time and a part-time job, continual juggling has to take place, partly to cherish the children and partly, with everybody getting ragged at the edges, to decide whether it is all worth it. Would it be possible to go down to one job again?

Priorities

So it is always a question of priorities and always, when we consider priorities, we come back to the question, How do we choose? Consider some of the following statements:

- 'A good smack doesn't do any harm.'
- 'Children need their mother most.'
- 'We go to lunch with the in-laws every other Sunday.'
- 'If a woman doesn't go out to work she becomes a cabbage.'
- 'We need a new suite in the sitting-room every five years.'
- 'The man's job comes first.'
- 'Children are resilient. We fuss about them too much.'
- 'I don't know why Tessa has to go out with the girls on a Friday night.'
- 'Of course we shall move to a bigger house as soon as we can.'
- 'No, I don't really like other people's children about the house.'

As you read these it wouldn't be surprising if you had some strong reactions. 'Yeah, too right!' 'Rubbish!' Such reactions will arise out of different sources. Some of the issues you might have thought about rather hard and then come to these conclusions. Others you will have accepted instinctively from your upbringing. 'My Dad's job always came first, so that's the way it is in my marriage.' Others again may have been a battleground between you and your spouse and you have stuck your heels in and agreed to differ, or your views have been shifted by the tussle.

Hidden within all the statements lie matters of precedence. Who or what comes first? Or rather, because only one thing or person can be first, in what order of precedence do we put our partner, our respective jobs, our children, our possessions, our family friends, our parents, our ambitions? As I say, some of this you will have hammered out with your partner and, before that, you will have learned much from your friends at school and maybe university. None of us has been alone in confronting some of the most difficult issues of our lives. But we are still left without any governing facts that can give us some idea of the proper direction to seek. It is as if we have been placed with all these people in a huge room with hundreds of different exits and we are all milling around trying to find the right way out.

It is possible to find such a governing factor; such can exist in some Code of Law, the Ten Commandments for example. Certainly the Ten Commandments, three thousand years old though they be, are a not insignificant guide to human conduct. If we take the Ten Commandments seriously we have to give some precedence to our parents ('Respect your father and your mother'), to our spouse ('Do not commit adultery,' *Exodus 20.14*) and to our neighbours ('Do not desire another man's house … or anything else that is his,' *Exodus 20.17*). Yet to follow this code or any other seems, and probably is, rather a cold sort of exercise. It is easy to spend our time measuring ourselves against the code and constantly discovering failure.

More inviting is to seek the God that lives behind the Ten Commandments. And once we have hit upon that idea it is tempting to ask God to show us which exit to take out of that perplexing room. He will not. God will only take us by the hand and say, 'Come,' expecting us to follow without surrendering an iota of our responsibility for the journey.

For some direction along our path, God has left us the Bible which records how active he has been in the history of the world. On several occasions in this book I have made reference to the Bible and particularly to the life and teaching of God's Son, Jesus. I think you will agree that on each occasion the quotations have been highly relevant to the contemporary issues I was discussing.

But more important, perhaps, in this business of sorting out who takes precedence over whom or what, is a lifelong attempt to allow ourselves to be led by God in prayer. For the fact is that, once we have understood that God precedes everybody and everything on earth (and prayer gradually allows us to see that) then after a time other priorities fall into place.

It can be of enormous value therefore if the family can do some learning about how to live by practising prayer. It is not simply an attempt to become holy (though I hope you might achieve that end rather than becoming pious). Prayer is also one of the ways in which we grow in understanding. Naturally many dawning understandings bring some trauma in their wake, but once that is surmounted we shall find that we have taken a further step towards harmony and love.

How exactly you pray is for each family to choose. Sunday worship, regularly undertaken, brings its own reward. At home some like to have regular family prayer, others would find that too embarrassing particularly as the children grow up. Prayer with younger children can be a natural practice at bed-time, and some couples have informal prayer together or say a quiet office like Compline in the late evening. If all this is too much, or too burdensome for your partner, the opportunities for private prayer will slowly bear fruit.

To do

Secrets
Hire the video of Mike Leigh's *Secrets and Lies*, a box-office success a few years ago that shows how secrets blockade a family but, once confronted, release it.

A Pearl of Great Price

After all the talk in these pages of pain and difficulty and hardship you might sigh and think to yourself, 'Is it all worth it?' Marriage is not for everybody. Some are called to a single life and, free of close family ties, often give themselves wonderfully to the world. Some marry with too little understanding of the nature of the task and quickly move away from their spouse, bewildered that so much was expected of them. Some marry with love and passion and great hopes for the future and only slowly come to understand what a dreadful mistake they have made, and leave their spouse with horror but relief. Some couples never get married at all and, as I have said before, the experiment of permanent cohabitation, even after the advent of children, is too recent a development for us to judge how over coming decades it will work out in practice. Many, after a divorce, remarry and the greater number find happiness the second time round, though the fallout from second marriages is at the moment even greater than for first marriages.

The Church, however, is not in the business of judgement. 'Judge not that you may not be judged,' said Jesus, 'for with the same judgement that you judge you yourself will be judged.' So when the Church condemns, it condemns only itself. Rather the Church, like its Master, is bidden to receive and care for all alike.

The Church is also commissioned to say to the world that for those who are called to it there is no condition more fruitful and enchanting than marriage. Many of us discover that, after many years, marriage seems to take on a life of its own. It claims the couple and binds them with a gentle yoke. I can end in no better way than to quote from a recent book by John Bayley. He was married for many decades to Iris Murdoch, the celebrated novelist, and wrote this book about their life together after she sank into the dark world of Alzheimer's disease. Neither of them was in any way a practising Christian though both were sympathetic to the life of the Spirit. Nevertheless he seems to have caught the essence of marriage in these words:

'Life is no longer bringing the pair of us "closer and closer apart", in the poet's tenderly ambiguous words. Every day we move closer and closer together. We could not do otherwise. There is a certain comic irony—happily not darkly comic—that after more than forty years of taking marriage for granted, marriage has decided it is tired of this, and is taking a hand in the game. Purposefully, persistently, involuntarily, our marriage is now getting somewhere. It is giving us no choice, and I am glad of that'.

Bayley J, *Iris: A Memoir* (Duckworth, 1999)